—Diseases and People—

ALZHEIMER'S DISEASE

Edward Willett

Enslow Publishers, Inc.

40 Industrial Road   PO Box 38
Box 398   Aldershot
Berkeley Heights, NJ 07922   Hants GU12 6BP
USA   UK

http://www.enslow.com

Library of Congress Cataloging-in-Publication Data

Willett, Edward, 1959-
     Alzheimer's disease / Edward Willett.
          p. cm. — (Diseases and people))
     Includes bibliographical references and index. Summary: Presents an overview of a degenerative brain disease which alters personality, memory, thinking and behavior and, at present, has no cure.
     ISBN 0-7660-1596-3
     1. Alzheimer's disease—Juvenile literature. [1. Alzheimer's disease.
     2. Diseases.] I. Title. II. Series.
     RC523.2 .W54 2002
     616.8'31—dc211   2001004517

Printed in the United States of America

10 9 8 7 6 5 4 3 2

To Our Readers:
We have done our best to make sure all Internet Addresses in this book were active and appropriate when we went to press. However, the author and the publisher have no control over and assume no liability for the material available on those Internet sites or on other Web sites they may link to. Any comments or suggestions can be sent by e-mail to comments@enslow.com or to the address on the back cover.

Illustration Credits: © Corel Corporation, pp. 23, 39, 47, 50, 75, 82, 87; Courtesy of Galerie Beckel Odille Boicos, p. 26 (both); Courtesy of Harvard Brain Tissue Resource Center, pp. 10, 11, 31; Díamar Interactive Corporation, p. 65; Illustration by Lydia Kibiuk, used with permission from the National Institute on Aging, p. 9; Images © 1995 Photo Disc, Inc., p. 47, 78, 82; National Archives, p. 25; National Institute on Aging, p. 14; National Library of Medicine, p. 18; Reproduced from the Collections of the Library of Congress, p. 16; UF Health Science Center, p. 44.

Cover Illustration: AP Photo/Bob Galbraith

Contents

ALZHEIMER'S DISEASE

What is it? Alzheimer's disease is a disorder of the brain that results in gradual mental deterioration. Eventually, the brain becomes so damaged that it can no longer properly regulate the body's many systems, and the patient dies. However, because this level of deterioration may take as long as twenty years to develop from the time the disease's symptoms are first noticed, Alzheimer's patients often die of other illnesses first.

Who gets it? Alzheimer's disease affects both men and women of all races. The older a person is, the more likely he or she is to have it. Alzheimer's disease is very rare in people under 50—a few people develop it between the ages of 45 and 55; most people who develop it are over 65. It is estimated to affect one in five people between the ages of 75 and 84—four million Americans—and nearly half of those 85 or older. People who develop Alzheimer's at a relatively young age generally have parents or other relatives who also succumbed to it at an early age. Head injuries, strokes, and brain infections can also make early development of Alzheimer's more likely.

How do you get it? The cause of Alzheimer's is not yet known. It is known that people with Alzheimer's exhibit two distinct changes in their brain cells: plaques and tangles. Plaques are made of a sticky protein called beta amyloid that builds up into small clumps in the cortex of the brain, intermingled with the functioning nerve cells. Tangles are made up of tau molecules, which normally form tiny tubes that support the structure of the brain cell. In Alzheimer's patients, the tau molecules change shape so that the tubes collapse and the cell shrinks and dies. Scientists don't yet know how these two changes in the brain take place or how they are related.

What are the symptoms? Alzheimer's disease is divided into three stages, with progressively worsening symptoms in each stage. In early-stage Alzheimer's, the symptoms include confusion about places; loss of initiative; decreased job performance because of a loss of recent memory; and mood and personality changes. Middle-stage symptoms include increasing memory loss and confusion; problems recognizing close friends; problems with reading, writing, and numbers; and an inability to find the right words. Finally, late-stage symptoms include weight loss; an inability to recognize family members or one's own image in a mirror; an inability to care for oneself; an inability to communicate; and loss of bowel and bladder control.

How is it treated? Currently, there are no cures for Alzheimer's. The drugs that are on the market for the disease boost the action of a brain chemical called acetylcholine. These drugs typically improve the patient's symptoms to where they were six months earlier. However, they do not work for all patients, and even when they do work, the symptoms eventually become so severe that a six-month improvement does not really help. Numerous new approaches to treatment are currently being researched, however, so new treatments will likely be available within the next few years.

Until then, the goal of those caring for Alzheimer's patients is to ensure their safety, comfort, and self-respect.

How can it be prevented? There is no known way of preventing Alzheimer's disease. However, there is some indication that antioxidants such as Vitamin E and anti-inflammatory drugs such as ibuprofen may reduce the risk of contracting it. Research also indicates that people who are better educated and keep their brains more active during their lives are less likely to develop Alzheimer's than poorer-educated, less mentally active people.

1

The Mind Thief

When Margaret was 68 years old, she started behaving strangely. She started leaving for work on certain days through the back door instead of the front. She packed a lunch for her grandson twice within a few minutes. She began to dress oddly—wearing shoes that did not match, forgetting to button her blouse all the way down, or choosing colors that clashed. She would grope for a simple word or lose track of what she was saying in the middle of a sentence. Although she had always been a gentle woman, she started becoming cranky when things did not go well, and even swore at the housekeeper.

When her daughter, Ann, who lived with her, expressed her concern about Margaret's behavior, Margaret was immediately offended and said she did not know what Ann was talking about. But as the mistakes and lapses grew worse over the weeks and months, Ann and three of Margaret's closest friends finally persuaded Margaret to see a doctor.

After a thorough checkup, a complete neurological examination, and an hour-long psychological test, the doctor told Ann that Margaret was suffering from dementia—most likely Alzheimer's disease.[1]

Dying by Inches

Alzheimer's disease is a progressive disease—it gets worse over time. It causes a deterioration of the brain, resulting in impaired memory, thinking, and behavior. It is a very frightening disease to most people because it alters personality, memory, thinking, and behavior—everything that makes us individuals. Eventually, it interferes with everyday activities and makes it impossible for a person to function independently. No wonder it is sometimes called "dying by inches."[2]

Although initially the person with Alzheimer's is aware that he or she is beginning to lose mental sharpness and may react with fear or anger, eventually the disease robs the patient of that awareness. After that, the family members, who must continue to ensure that the patient is cared for long after he or she can even recognize or respond to them, also become victims.[3]

When Alzheimer's disease was first identified in 1906, it was considered very rare. As life expectancy has increased, however (from 47 years in 1906 to 77 years in 1999), Alzheimer's has become increasingly common. That is because

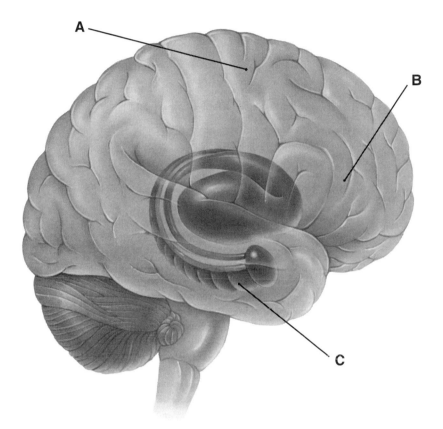

Alzheimer's disease attacks nerve cells in the cerebral cortex (A), the basal forebrain (B), and the hippocampus (C). The cerebral cortex is involved in conscious thought and language. The basal forebrain is important in memory and learning. The hippocampus is essential to memory storage.

Alzheimer's is primarily a disease of old age, afflicting one in five people aged 75 to 84 and nearly half of those 85 and older.[4] Only a small percentage of people under 65 get the disease, but from age 65 on, the number of cases doubles with every five years of age.[5]

Difficult to Diagnose, Impossible to Cure

Alzheimer's is difficult to diagnose because there is no one test that indicates that a person is afflicted with it. It is only one of many forms of dementia. The word "dementia" comes from the Latin words *de*, meaning "from," and *mentis*, meaning "mind." A person with dementia is no longer in his or her normal state of mind. Dementia can be caused by everything from strokes to medication to brain injuries. In fact, doctors estimate that more than sixty different disorders can produce dementia—but Alzheimer's is far more common than any other cause.[6]

To diagnose Alzheimer's, the doctor has to rule out many of the other possible causes of dementia. Even then, he can only say that a particular patient most likely has Alzheimer's (because he or she apparently does not have one of the other forms of dementia, so Alzheimer's is all that is left). The only way to be absolutely certain that someone had Alzheimer's is to

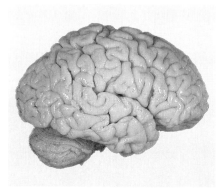

A normal brain is pictured here.

examine his or her brain under a microscope after death.

Such an examination will reveal two major differences between the brain of someone who had Alzheimer's and someone who did not. These two changes are called amyloid plaques and neurofibrillary tangles.

Amyloid plaques are sticky deposits formed from a naturally occurring protein called beta amyloid protein, or BAP. People with Alzheimer's seem to make too much of this protein, compared to people without Alzheimer's.[7]

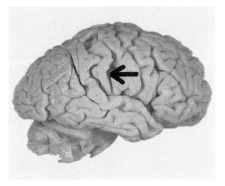

This photograph of a brain affected by Alzheimer's shows how the disease has destroyed areas of brain tissue. The arrow points to one of the deep grooves that is a sign of the brain's deterioration, a distinctive indication of the disease.

Neurofibrillary tangles are made up of tau proteins, which ordinarily reinforce important structures in brain cells called microtubules, holding them together like the crosspieces in a stretch of railroad track. In people with Alzheimer's, these tau proteins have broken loose to form tangles. Without tau proteins reinforcing them, the microtubules disintegrate and the whole brain cell withers and dies.[8]

Although scientists know that these changes occur in the brains of people with Alzheimer's, they are still not sure whether the buildup of plaques and the formation of tangles are the cause of Alzheimer's, or just one of its symptoms.

Partly because the cause of Alzheimer's still is not known, there is currently no cure for it. Only four drugs have so far been approved to treat Alzheimer's. Tacrine (brand name Cognex®), donepezil (brand name Aricept®), rivastigmine (brand name Exelon®), and galantamine (brand name Reminyl®) all ease the symptoms of the disease by inhibiting the breakdown of a brain chemical called acetylcholine, which is vital for nerve cells to communicate with each other. The longer acetylcholine remains in the brain, the longer nerve cells can call up memories.[9] These drugs are not a cure, and some patients do not respond to them at all. The effectiveness of the drugs in those patients who do respond to them is demonstrated by the fact that the patients experience a rapid decline in mental ability once they stop using them.[10]

Research is continuing at a frantic pace and new discoveries are announced almost every month. There is hope on the horizon that new drugs may be able to slow or even stop the progression of Alzheimer's disease, turning it into an illness something like heart disease: serious, but something that can be treated and possibly prevented.[11]

Doctors hope that is true, because Alzheimer's is already a very serious problem, and it is going to become even more serious over the next few years.

An Imminent Worldwide Epidemic

Currently, it is estimated that twenty million people suffer from the disease worldwide—four million in the United States alone. As life expectancies continue to increase and the world population grows, those numbers will also mushroom. According to Edward Truschke, president of the Alzheimer's Association, more than 22 million people could have the disease worldwide by 2025, which makes it "an imminent worldwide epidemic." Dr. Robert Katzman of the University of California, San Diego, estimates the total could be 45 million worldwide by 2050—as many people as suffer from all types of cancer.[12]

The impact of the disease on society is staggering for several reasons. The sheer number of sufferers is one. Related to that number is the fact that more than seven out of ten people with Alzheimer's disease live at home, and almost 75 percent of home care is provided by family and friends.[13] That pattern of involvement expands the circle of those affected by Alzheimer's enormously.

The other impact on society comes from the enormous cost of caring for Alzheimer's patients. The 25 percent of care that is not directly provided by family and friends is usually paid for, at an average cost of $12,500 per year. The average lifetime cost of caring for an Alzheimer's patient is $174,000. The cost of Alzheimer's to American businesses each year is estimated at $33 billion ($26 billion due to the lost productivity of the people caring for Alzheimer's patients and $7 billion related to costs for health and long-term care). The total cost to the United States alone each year is estimated at $100 billion.[14]

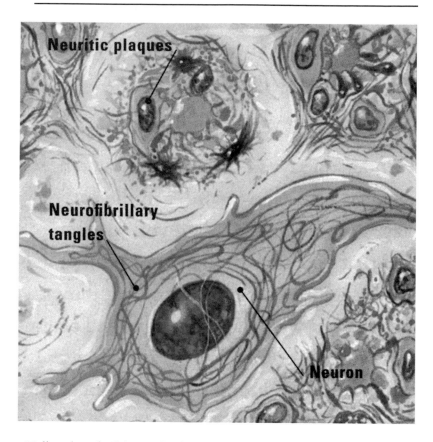

Hallmarks of Alzheimer's disease include neuritic plaques (outside neurons), and neurofibrillary tangles (inside neurons).

The increasing numbers of Alzheimer's patients mean that if you do not currently know someone who suffers from Alzheimer's or has a family member who does, you almost certainly will in the years to come. This makes it all the more important that you understand as much as you can about the disease, its effects—and the current hopes that more effective treatment may not be too far away.

14

2
The History of Alzheimer's Disease

Few scientists' names are more immediately recognizable than that of Alois Alzheimer, because of the disease that is named after him. But it is interesting to note that it has only been in the last thirty years or so that his name has become such a familiar part of the language. Before that, the disease he discovered was considered an oddity that was only recognized in relatively young patients under 60.

Of course, dementia, or "feeble-mindedness" related to advanced age, has been known throughout history. For example, there are records of chronic forgetfulness among elderly people in Egypt dating back to the ninth century B.C., and Claudius Galen, a Roman doctor who lived between A.D. 130–200, recounted symptoms of age-related forgetfulness in his writing.

Claudius Galen, a Roman doctor who lived between A.D. 130–200, recounted symptoms of age-related forgetfulness in his writing.

From medieval England, there is even a record of a test given to a woman named Emma de Beston in Cambridge in 1383 that is remarkably similar to tests given today to screen for the early symptoms of Alzheimer's. The test asked such questions as, "What town are you living in?", "How many husbands do you have?", and "How many days are in a week?"[1]

In the 1600s, forgetfulness was considered an unavoidable part of aging and was assumed to be the work of witches or the devil. In the 1700s, the senile elderly who could not be hidden away at home were confined to hospitals for the insane. (One such infamous asylum, Bethlehem Royal, just outside of London, became known as "Bedlam.")

It was not until the 1800s that anyone approached senility in the elderly scientifically. In 1838, French doctors first suggested that changes in the minds of elderly people had to be caused by something separate from mental retardation and insanity, because the people who became senile had not always been that way.[2] But it was not until Alois Alzheimer came along that anyone discovered exactly what changes were occurring in the minds of people who suffered from dementia in their old age.

Alzheimer was born in 1864 in Markbreit, Germany, where his father was a civil servant. As a young man, Alzheimer studied medicine in Berlin and Tübingen, and graduated in Würzburg. He received his medical degree in 1887 at the age of 23. His doctoral thesis, far from being concerned with diseases of the brain, focused on the glands that produce ear wax.[3]

17

Alois Alzheimer first identified the disease in 1907, and distinguished psychiatrist Emil Kraepelin proposed naming the condition after its discoverer.

Upon receiving his medical degree, Alzheimer was appointed a clinical assistant at the asylum in Frankfurt, where he worked with neurologist Franz Nissl, researching the pathology of the nervous system. Together, he and Nissl published the six-volume reference work *Histologic and Histopathologic Studies of the Cerebral Cortex*, which appeared between 1904 and 1918.[4]

It was while he was working in the asylum in Frankfurt that Alzheimer came across a patient by the name of Auguste D., who was prone to angry outbursts and fits of paranoia. Sometimes she would pat the faces of other people, apparently mistaking their faces for her own.[5]

Auguste D. was 51 years old when Alzheimer met her. She died just four and a half years later. Alzheimer performed an autopsy on her and studied her brain tissue under a microscope using a new technique, silver impregnation, to stain the brain cells. With the staining, he was able to identify striking differences between her brain cells and those of a normal brain. Specifically, he noticed that many nerve cells had vanished and had been replaced by tangled masses, and that other cells were coated with fatty deposits. Noted Alzheimer, "Apparently we are dealing with an unidentified illness."[6]

Other doctors agreed, and Emil Kraepelin, a distinguished psychiatrist, proposed naming the new condition after its discoverer, Alois Alzheimer.[7]

In addition to his research on dementia, Alzheimer made important observations concerning other illnesses, including

Alzheimer's Disease in Alzheimer's Own Words

In his 1907 article "A new disease of the cortex," Alois Alzheimer described the symptoms of the patient in which he first identified the disease in these words:

The case had presented with such varied symptoms that it defied classification under existing illnesses and had pathological findings different from any process so far known.

The first sign was an unfounded morbid jealousy of her husband. Then came rapid onset amnesia to the point where she became lost in her own home, carried objects aimlessly around, hid them. She felt she was about to be murdered and had spells of unrestrained screaming.[8]

When committed to the institution, her behavior was dominated by total helplessness. She was confused as to time and place. Occasionally she remarked that she did not understand anything and did not know her way about. At times she was delirious, and carried parts of her bed around, calling for her husband and daughter, and had auditory hallucinations. Often she screamed in a frightening voice for hours at a time.

Her walk was normal and unhampered, patellar reflexes were present, and the pupils reacted. Mental deterioration progressed and she died 4 1/2 years later. By then she showed little response, remained in bed with her legs drawn to her body, neglected herself, and, in spite of all nursing, developed decubitus (bedsores).[9]

epilepsy, brain tumors, and alcoholic delirium. In 1912, the University of Breslau appointed Alzheimer professor of psychiatry and director of the Psychiatric and Neurologic Institute. Alzheimer continued his research there for three years, but died of heart disease in 1915 at the age of 51.[10]

Although Alzheimer's discovery attracted scientific interest at the time, the disease was generally considered rare for many decades thereafter. That was because Alzheimer had discovered it in an unusually young patient. As a result, doctors thought that Alzheimer's disease only afflicted relatively young patients. Older patients who suffered from the same symptoms were said to have "senile dementia," which was thought to be something else entirely.

As the twentieth century progressed, however, life expectancy increased greatly, from just 47 years when Alzheimer identified the disease to more than 77 years today.[11] As a result, more cases of "senile dementia" were observed.

In 1968, G. Blessed, B. E. Tomlinson, and M. Roth published a paper in the British Journal of Psychiatry entitled "The association between quantitative measures of dementia and of senile change in the cerebral gray matter of elderly subjects," which for the first time made the connection between senile dementia and Alzheimer's, establishing that, for the most part, they were the same disease.[12]

Doctors did not get any closer to curing or treating the disease, but it began to attract more and more attention as the number of cases mounted. A number of support groups for families whose loved ones had Alzheimer's were formed, and in

1979, representatives from five of those groups met to discuss the possibility of forming a national Alzheimer's association. The groups then met in Washington, D.C., with Dr. Richard Butler, who was then the director of the National Institute on Aging, and agreed to form what today is known as the Alzheimer's Association.[13]

Awareness of the disease continued to grow. In 1983, the United States Congress declared November "National Alzheimer's Disease Month" for the first time, and President Ronald Reagan approved the creation of a task force to oversee and coordinate scientific research into Alzheimer's disease. That research bore fruit in 1984, when it finally revealed the structure of beta-amyloid protein, the sticky substance that clumps to form the plaques that Alzheimer noted in 1907.[14]

Three years later, the gene responsible for amyloid precursor protein (APP), which breaks down to form the beta-amyloid protein that forms Alzheimer's plaques, was sequenced by researchers. This was funded in part by the young Alzheimer's Association.

These discoveries were the beginning of an explosion of knowledge about how Alzheimer's disease attacks the brain. "We've learned more in the past 15 years than in the previous 85," says Dr. Bruce Yankner of Harvard Medical School.[15]

The discovery of a gene that tells cells how to make the protein which becomes beta amyloid protein led to more research into the genetics of Alzheimer's. In 1991, scientists at London's St. Mary's Hospital Medical School discovered a mutant version of the gene that can lead to early-onset Alzheimer's in some patients. Early-onset Alzheimer's begins before age 65. This accounts for less than one percent of all cases.[16]

Two more early-onset genes were found shortly thereafter: Presenilin-1 and Presenilin-2. But they, too, only account for a small number of Alzheimer's cases—about 4 percent in the case of Presenilin-1 and about one percent in the case of Presenilin-2.[17]

In 1983, President Ronald Reagan approved the creation of the task force to oversee and coordinate scientific research into Alzheimer's disease.

In 1992, Dr. Allen Roses, then at Duke University, announced that he and his colleagues had found another gene that makes people more susceptible to Alzheimer's: Apolipoprotein E4, or ApoE4. It appears in about 65 percent of Alzheimer's patients—but not everyone who has it develops the disease, so testing for it is mainly used in population studies and to provide additional evidence in diagnosing Alzheimer's.[18] Research continues into other genes that could make people susceptible to Alzheimer's.

In the meantime, much of the debate in the last five years has centered on whether beta-amyloid protein or tau protein plays the central role in the disease—or if some other cause produces both plaques and tangles.

With more being learned about Alzheimer's every day, it is safe to say that much of the history of the disease is being written now.

No One is Immune

It is ironic to note that Ronald Reagan was the president who first approved the creation of a task force to coordinate research into Alzheimer's disease. In 1994, he was diagnosed with Alzheimer's disease.

His daughter Maureen remembered the first time she realized something was wrong. "It was late in 1993 and we were having dinner with my father," she wrote. "We were discussing a 1950s film he made, *Prisoner of War*. For years he had told me about the gruesome tortures inflicted on American prisoners by the North Koreans. But now he seemed to be hearing me tell the stories for the first time. Finally he looked at me and said, 'Mermie, I have no recollection of making that movie.'"[19]

By age 89, he no longer even remembered being president.

Alzheimer's has affected many other celebrities over the years. Rita Hayworth, an actress once known as "The Great American Love Goddess" and one of the top movie stars of the 1940s and 1950s, died on May 14, 1987 of Alzheimer's disease at the age of 69. She suffered from the disease for 15 years. Her last film was 1972's *The Wrath of God.*

Another actor afflicted with Alzheimer's was Burgess Meredith, probably best known as Rocky's trainer in the first *Rocky* movie (1976) and as the Penguin in the 1960s TV series "Batman." Despite suffering from Alzheimer's, he continued working, with the help of cue cards, right up until his death in 1997 at the age of 89.

E. B. White, author of the classic children's books *Stuart Little, Charlotte's Web,* and *The Trumpet of the Swan,* suffered from Alzheimer's. He eventually lost his ability to work with words and died in 1988 at the age of 86. Aaron Copland, one of the most influential American composers of the twentieth century, died of Alzheimer's in 1990 at the age of 90.

Actress Rita Hayworth suffered from Alzheimer's disease for 15 years before her death in 1987.

William Utermohlen

Not many artists can say that their self-portraits have been the focus of an academic paper published in the distinguished British medical journal *The Lancet*, but William Utermohlen can.

Utermohlen, known for his portraits and murals, was diagnosed with Alzheimer's disease in 1997 at age 62. He continued painting self-portraits for several more years before abandoning painting for good.

The self-portraits show increasing distortion, some of which Utermohlen probably intended—enlarged ears in one self-portrait to reflect hearing problems, for instance— but most of which was the result of declining coordination and spatial awareness.

By continuing to paint self-portraits after his diagnosis, Utermohlen gave Alzheimer's researchers a unique tool to study how the progressive decline caused by the disease feels from the inside.

"It is difficult for people with progressive cognitive impairment to talk about their experience," says Martin Rossor, co-author of *The Lancet* and vice-president of the Alzheimer's Society. "This is a very direct way for him to speak about it."

Athletes, too, are included in the long list of Alzheimer's patients. Sugar Ray Robinson, five-time world middleweight champion boxer, considered by many experts to be the best fighter of all time, was suffering from Alzheimer's when he died in 1989.

Politicians, actors, writers, musicians, athletes, and "ordinary" people—no one is immune to the ravages of Alzheimer's disease.

3

What Is Alzheimer's Disease?

Anson P. Hobbs was an industrial research chemist living in Pittsburgh and knew nothing about Alzheimer's disease when he first noticed his wife, Mildred, doing peculiar things for which he had no explanation. He started taking her to a doctor for monthly check-ups. He would schedule a checkup at the same time, but would send her in first so the doctor could tell him what he had found. The doctor did not know for sure what the trouble was.

Then, the Hobbs' children told their father that the letters their mother wrote them had lines running in all directions and did not make sense. When they talked to her, she would at first appear to be all right, but then would change subjects and stop making sense.

Anson noticed that when she wrote her name, she would keep putting loops in the "M" until he told her to stop.

She could not cook any more because she would forget what she was doing.

The doctor ran a brain scan and said that Mildred was suffering from "atrophy of the brain cells." Shortly after that, the couple moved to a retirement village in Tulsa, Oklahoma. By then, Mildred had to be with Anson constantly because she could no longer take care of herself. The couple joined a church choir but had to quit because Mildred could no longer follow instructions.

Anson continued to take her to a doctor for monthly exams. Eventually, she was sent to a neurologist, who diagnosed her with Alzheimer's disease. Anson began to read everything he could about the disease but for the first time had to face the fact that Mildred would not get any better.

Over the next few years, Mildred continued to deteriorate. She could not read. She could not knit. She could not even go to the bathroom without her husband's help. Eventually, Anson was feeding her, bathing her, dressing and undressing her, helping her out of bed and back into bed—he was doing everything just as if she were a child. Sometimes, she became violent.

Finally, Anson was forced to put Mildred, to whom he had been married for 44 years, into the health center. She lived for five more years, but eventually could no longer recognize her husband or her children, who did not want to see her because they wanted to remember her as she was before.

Mildred Hobbs died on January 6, 1986.[1]

Progressive and Degenerative

Alzheimer's disease is a progressive, degenerative brain disease, and the leading cause of dementia in America.

"Progressive" means that the disease gets worse over time. "Degenerative" means that it causes the brain to deteriorate, or slowly fail.

Alzheimer's disease usually begins gradually and the speed at which it advances varies from person to person. Over time, it impairs brain functioning to the extent that the person with Alzheimer's disease is no longer able to care for him- or herself.[2]

The deterioration of brain functioning is caused by the death of nerve cells in the brain. Scientists do not yet know for sure what causes the disease, but they are learning more and more about how the damage to the brain occurs.

As Alois Alzheimer noticed when he first described the disease back in 1907, brain cells in patients with Alzheimer's show two distinct types of damage: plaques and tangles.

Perilous Plaques

The plaques are sticky deposits of a protein called beta amyloid. Even normal cells make this protein. It is formed from another protein called amyloid precursor protein, or APP. Cells use enzymes called secretases on their surface to make beta amyloid out of APP. The secretases act like scissors, snipping beta amyloid from the larger APP molecules.

Normally, beta amyloid protein dissolves after it drifts away from the nerve cell that formed it, but when an abnormal secretase "ships" the APP to a different location, it forms up into insoluble clumps called fibrils. These fibrils cluster together with other fibrils, eventually creating the plaques seen in Alzheimer's patients.

Even people who do not develop Alzheimer's create some of these plaques as they get older. In Alzheimer's patients, however, these plaques cause inflammation, just like an infection would. Over time, this inflammation, which normally functions to kill viruses and bacteria but does nothing to remove the plaques, destroys brain cells in the vicinity of the plaques.[3]

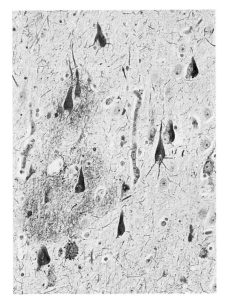

This microscopic view shows the neurons and plaques (dark fuzzy areas) found in the brain of a person with Alzheimer's disease. The plaques and the tangled filaments (contained in the black-colored neurons) are indications that the brain cells are dead or dying.

Among the weapons the brain unleashes so uselessly against the plaques are special cells called miroglia and toxic molecules called oxygen-free radicals. Like tiny garbage collectors, the miroglia keep trying the clear the plaques away, while the oxygen-free radicals try to poison them. Neither works, but both can eventually damage healthy cells.[4]

Terrible Tangles

The tangles that show up in the brains of people with Alzheimer's are formed by another protein called tau. A healthy brain cell looks kind of like a squid or an octopus, with long tentacle-like appendages that reach out and link to other brain cells. These tentacles, or neurites, are built around structures called microtubules, which give the brain cell its shape and transport nutrients and the chemicals the cells use to communicate internally and with other cells. Tau proteins hold the microtubules together, reinforcing them like ties on a railroad track.

In Alzheimer's patients, for some reason, enzymes attack tau, loosening it from the sides of the microtubules. As a result, the tau proteins break loose, and instead of reinforcing the microtubules, tangle together uselessly. Without tau proteins to reinforce them, the microtubules fall apart, collapsing into messy clumps called neurofibrillary tangles.[5]

The big question scientists are currently trying to answer is: Which plays a larger role in causing Alzheimer's, the plaques or the tangles? Does one cause the other? Is either one the primary cause of Alzheimer's, or are they both the result of some other, as yet unknown, process that really causes the disease?

Some scientists think that beta amyloid plaques are the primary cause of Alzheimer's. (In the field of Alzheimer's research, they're known as "Baptists." The name has nothing to do with their religious beliefs—the first three letters, BAP, stand for beta amyloid protein.)[6] They think that the amyloid

32

plaques cause the tau proteins to tangle up by pressing up against the outer surfaces of brain cells, starting a series of chemical reactions that eventually detaches the proteins from the microtubules. Scientists know that an enzyme called cdk5 is what causes tau to tear loose, but they still do not know for sure what causes the brain cells to produce that self-destructive enzyme.[7]

Some scientists (called "Tauists"—a play on the word Taoist) believe that the tangles of tau protein are the primary cause of Alzheimer's. Others think that something else altogether—maybe a problem with the way the body forms proteins—may be the cause of both the plaques and the tangles.[8]

Research underway as this book was being written may provide the final answer within just a few years.

Three Stages of Symptoms

Although the rate at which Alzheimer's disease develops varies from person to person, it tends to follow the same pattern in everyone. A patient with the disease moves through three stages: mild, moderate, and severe.

Mild

In the first, mild stage, the symptoms are subtle, which is why people with the disease and those around them do not immediately realize that anything is wrong.[9]

Asking the same question over and over, losing things, forgetting appointments or birthdays, or forgetting to pay bills are common symptoms at this stage. At first, many people are able to use calendars and lists to remind themselves of what they have to do, but eventually these techniques do not work anymore.

The patient can still manage independently, but things that were once easy to do become much harder and learning new information becomes more difficult. To make things worse, the person having these kinds of problems often will not admit that the problems exist, and may resist going to the doctor or seeking any other kind of help.[10]

Other symptoms of first-stage Alzheimer's include confusion about places, a loss of initiative, mood and personality changes, a tendency to avoid people, and a tendency to make bad decisions. Memory problems will typically begin to affect job performance.[11]

Patients will begin to forget names for simple things like bread or butter and may have trouble recognizing what numbers mean. This is one way to distinguish between the kind of memory loss brought on by Alzheimer's and the kind of absent-mindedness everyone suffers from time to time when they cannot remember where they put something.[12]

The first stage of Alzheimer's generally lasts from two to four years, but can even last up to ten years.[13]

Moderate

In the second, moderate stage of Alzheimer's, the symptoms get worse. The patient now needs supervision in order to function even in familiar surroundings, but can still respond to simple directions. Any sort of complex task involving a series of steps—such as getting dressed or cooking a meal—becomes more difficult.

Memory loss is no longer helped by reminders such as lists or calendars, and can even include forgetting to eat. Patients begin to lose a sense of social conventions, so they may, for example, wear a bathrobe to the park or otherwise dress inappropriately. They may become confused about what time it is or where they are.

All these problems can put the patient at risk, because he or she may get lost, drive dangerously, leave the stove on, or mix up medications. To make matters worse, the patient often can no longer understand what is happening, and as a result may resist being helped or blame others for problems. More and more supervision is needed and eventually, constant supervision is required.[14]

Patients may have trouble recognizing close friends, may repeat themselves, will often have trouble reading and writing, and may even suffer from hallucinations (seeing or hearing things that are not there). They may start twitching or jerking and have trouble walking normally. They may refuse to bathe.[15]

The second stage of Alzheimer's typically lasts from two to eight years.[16]

Severe

Finally, in the last stage of Alzheimer's, memory loss and confusion become so severe that the patient no longer recognizes family members. Walking, standing, or even getting out of a chair becomes difficult, which makes falling a constant risk. Patients may lose control of their bowels or bladders. They may lose the ability to swallow solids or even liquids, and as a result may become malnourished and dehydrated.

They may become extremely suspicious of people, have trouble sleeping, have difficulty talking or stop talking altogether, and may suffer seizures.[17] Besides not recognizing others, they may even be unable to recognize themselves in a mirror.[18]

Eventually, the Alzheimer's patient becomes bedridden and needs twenty-four-hour care until death.

Once a patient enters the severe phase, he or she usually lives only one to three more years.[19]

4

Diagnosing Alzheimer's Disease

Mike Crowe of Penticton, British Columbia, Canada, had worked for the same company for twenty-five years and had only eight years to go until retirement when, in June of 1995, he received an unwelcome letter from his employer: "Sorry we have to let you go. There are just too many problems affecting your work. Perhaps you should see a doctor. You might have a medical problem."

Crowe was forgetting deadlines and appointments at work, and making a lot of mistakes. At home, he was exhausted and withdrawn, reading the newspaper, watching TV, and not talking much. Both he and his wife, Nora, attributed it to stress. But in fact, the symptoms Crowe was exhibiting—memory loss, difficulty performing tasks, mood changes, loss of initiative—are among the warning signs of early Alzheimer's disease.

In January, 1997, Mike Crowe was diagnosed with the disease.[1]

The Importance of Early Diagnosis

In the early stages, Alzheimer's disease is easy to misinterpret, just like Mike and Nora Crowe did. It may be assumed to be depression or just normal aging. Yet early diagnosis is important because other conditions and problems besides Alzheimer's can also cause dementia, and many of them can be treated.

"Where the dementia is caused by a reversible condition, the earlier you detect it, the more chance you have of reversing it," says Dr. Howard Bergman, director of Montreal's Jewish General Hospital/McGill University Memory Clinic.[2]

And even though Alzheimer's itself cannot be reversed, earlier diagnosis gives the patient and his or her family more time to prepare for the changes ahead as the disease takes its course. It also provides more opportunity to attempt to slow the progression of the disease with the drugs that are now available.[3]

"If an early diagnosis of Alzheimer's disease can be obtained, it allows families to start planning for the future—discussing financial arrangements, living arrangements, making sure they have the necessary support services," says Dr. Michael Cooper, a geriatric psychiatrist at Penticton Regional Hospital in British Columbia. "If Alzheimer's medication can lead to a better quality of life," adds Dr. Cooper, "then doctors will want to discuss it with patients and their families at an early stage."[4]

Everyone becomes a bit more forgetful as they get older. But the forgetfulness brought on by early Alzheimer's is much more severe than just forgetting where you put your car keys. "It reaches into people's lives to affect their reasoning, memory, concentration, and use of language," Dr. Mary Gorman, consultant to the geriatric assessment and rehabilitation unit of St. Martha's Regional Hospital in Antigonish, Nova Scotia, says. "It affects people's ability to interpret the world in space and in thought."[5]

To help people better determine if someone should see a doctor, the Alzheimer's Association has developed a list of warning signs to watch for (see pages 42–43). Anyone with several of the symptoms should see a physician for a complete examination.

Everyone becomes a bit more forgetful as they get older, but the forgetfulness brought on by Alzheimer's disease is much more severe than just misplacing your car keys.

The Alzheimer's Association's Ten Warning Signs of Alzheimer's Disease[6]

1. **Memory loss that affects job skills.** It's normal to occasionally forget an assignment, deadline, or colleague's name, but frequent forgetfulness or unexplainable confusion at home or in the workplace may signal that something's wrong.

2. **Difficulty performing familiar tasks.** Busy people get distracted from time to time. For example, you might leave something on the stove too long or not remember to serve part of a meal. People with Alzheimer's might prepare a meal and not only forget to serve it but also forget they made it.

3. **Problems with language.** Everyone has trouble finding the right word sometimes, but a person with Alzheimer's disease may forget simple words or substitute inappropriate words, making his or her sentences difficult to understand.

4. **Disorientation to time and place.** It's normal to momentarily forget the day of the week or what you need from the store. But people with Alzheimer's disease can become lost on their own street, not knowing where they are, how they got there, or how to get back home.

5. **Poor or decreased judgment.** Choosing not to bring a sweater or coat along on a chilly night is a common mistake. A person with Alzheimer's, however,

may dress inappropriately in more noticeable ways, wearing a bathrobe to the store or several blouses on a hot day.

6. **Problems with abstract thinking.** Balancing a check book can be challenging for many people, but for someone with Alzheimer's, recognizing numbers or performing basic calculation may be impossible.

7. **Misplacing things.** Everyone temporarily misplaces a wallet or keys from time to time. A person with Alzheimer's disease may put these and other items in inappropriate places—such as an iron in the freezer or a wristwatch in the sugar bowl—and then not recall how they got there.

8. **Changes in mood or behavior.** Everyone experiences a broad range of emotions—it's part of being human. People with Alzheimer's tend to exhibit more rapid mood swings for no apparent reason.

9. **Changes in personality.** People's personalities may change somewhat as they age. But a person with Alzheimer's can change dramatically, either suddenly or over a period of time. Someone who is generally easygoing may become angry, suspicious, or fearful.

10. **Loss of initiative.** It's normal to tire of housework, business activities, or social obligations, but most people retain or eventually regain their interest. The person with Alzheimer's disease may remain uninterested and uninvolved in many or all of his usual pursuits.

Much of that examination will be aimed at ruling out other possible causes of the symptoms. There are dozens of conditions that can mimic Alzheimer's disease, including depression, interactions among prescription drugs, drug overdoses, dehydration, anemia, syphilis, viral infections, vitamin deficiencies, thyroid problems, and strokes.[7]

The First Step: Medical History

As with any disease, the first step toward diagnosis is a complete medical history. The doctor tries to find out what the person's current mental and physical condition is, what prescription drugs he or she is taking, and if there are any health problems that may run in the family.[8]

Next, the doctor will usually evaluate the person's mental status. He might, for example, administer a test in which the patient would be asked questions such as "What year is it now?", "What month is it now?", and "About what time is it?" The patient may also be asked to repeat a phrase back, count backwards from twenty to one, and say the months in reverse order.

Another test measures how dependent someone has become on others by asking how easily he or she is able to perform various activities, such as paying bills, shopping for clothes, preparing a meal, driving, or preparing a balanced meal.[9] There are many other tests similar to these, all designed to test memory, reasoning, language, and functional ability.

Next comes a complete physical examination, including an evaluation of the patient's nutritional status, blood pressure and pulse. Detailed blood and urine tests are ordered to help detect problems such as anemia, diabetes, thyroid problems, or infections that might be causing the symptoms. A neurological examination, which tests the nervous system for signs of other neurological disorders, often follows. Sometimes, a magnetic resonance imaging (MRI) scan of the brain can reveal signs of other things that could be causing dementia, such as a brain tumor or stroke; it usually does not show anything unusual at all in patients with early-stage Alzheimer's.

Various other tests, such as a psychiatric evaluation, may also be carried out.[10]

Probable, Possible, or Definite

Eventually, the doctor has to make a diagnosis. If he does diagnose Alzheimer's disease, he will typically characterize the diagnosis as either probable or possible.

A diagnosis of probable Alzheimer's means that he has ruled out all the other disorders he can think of that might be causing the diagnosis, leaving Alzheimer's as the most likely cause of the symptoms. Typically, this diagnosis indicates an 80 to 90 percent certainty.

A diagnosis of possible Alzheimer's means that he thinks Alzheimer's is the main cause of the symptoms, but that there could be some other physical problem affecting the way it

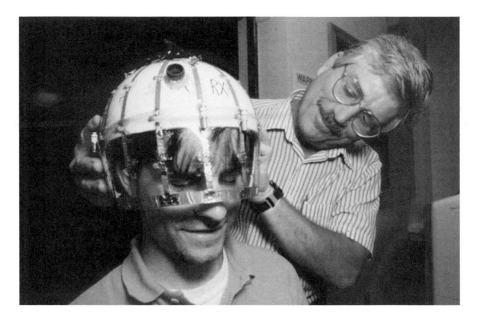

A magnetic resonance imaging (MRI) scan of the brain can reveal signs of other things that could be causing dementia, such as a brain tumor or stroke. Here, University of Florida radiologist Jeffrey Fitzsimmons positions a modified football helmet on a volunteer's head in preparation for an MRI scan.

progresses. Usually, a diagnosis of "possible" Alzheimer's indicates a certainty of about 60 percent.

A diagnosis of definite Alzheimer's can only be made for a patient who is no longer living, because it requires an autopsy and microscopic examination of tissue from the brain, revealing those same plaques and tangles that Alois Alzheimer first saw so many decades ago when he discovered the disease.[11]

5

Treatment of Alzheimer's Disease

Early one morning, Allen Scott, 62, of Lawrenceville, New Jersey, went for an early-morning stroll to take care of an errand. But halfway across a busy highway intersection—an intersection he had crossed dozens of times—he became mesmerized by the bright rays of the rising sun and forgot where he was or why he was there. He froze, paralyzed with fear.

He eventually made it to the other side of the road, but he knew something was wrong. "When you lose yourself out in the middle of U.S. 1, and the sun won't let you move, you know you're in trouble," says Scott. "I had no idea what that was. I had no idea how to deal with it."

Scott went to a doctor, who eventually diagnosed Alzheimer's disease.

Over the next three years, Scott taught himself many different techniques to get through each day. He also takes a number of drugs on a daily basis. He is trying to live a normal life as long as he can. Among other things, he attends a monthly support group run by the Central New Jersey branch of the Alzheimer's Association, where he suggests ways for other patients to deal with their mental impairments.[1]

Scott's situation is typical of many Alzheimer's patients today. Greater awareness of the disease means that people are being diagnosed with it earlier than ever before and can deal with it better, as well as make the most effective use of the few drugs that are available to treat it.

Nevertheless, the fact remains that there are currently no drugs or other medical treatments that can slow or halt the progression of the disease; they can only help patients deal with the symptoms. The focus of most treatment is teaching Alzheimer's patients and their loved ones to cope with the disease, not to cure it.

Treating Cognitive Symptoms

Alzheimer's disease produces two kinds of symptoms. It changes the ability of the person with the disease to think and reason and it changes the way that person acts. The first type of symptom is called *cognitive* and the second *behavioral*. Both types of symptoms need to be treated.

To treat the decline in cognitive ability, doctors currently have only four approved drugs in the United States. Tacrine (brand name Cognex®), has been available since 1993;

The Food and Drug Administration, the governing body responsible for approving drugs for use in the United States, has currently approved four drugs to be used in the treatment of Alzheimer's disease.

donepezil (brand name Aricept®), has been available since 1996; and rivastigmine (brand name Exelon®), was approved in 2000. Galantamine (brand name Reminyl®) was approved in 2001 by the Food and Drug Administration, the government body responsible for approving drugs for use in the United States.[2]

None of these drugs do anything to halt the progression of the disease. Instead, they increase the brain's supply of acetyl-choline, a chemical that brain cells use to communicate with each other. People with Alzheimer's have a shortage of acetylcholine.

The newest drug, galantamine, which was approved in March of 2001, makes brain cells more receptive to acetyl-choline as well as boosts the brain's supply.[3]

Although all four drugs can ease some of the cognitive problems of Alzheimer's patients, some patients do not respond at all to them. Even in the patients who do respond to them, the change is usually only an improvement to the condition the patient was in six months prior.

William Van Zandt of Middletown, N.J., started taking donepezil two years after he was diagnosed with Alzheimer's, and his family noticed an immediate difference. "He went from being completely uncommunicative to forming whole sentences," recalls his son, Billy. "My brother and sister called up in tears, saying, 'We've got the cure.'"

But just eight weeks later, Van Zandt started to decline again. After six months, the family dropped the drug because the benefit no longer seemed worthwhile.[4]

Some Facts About Alzheimer's Drugs[5]

Tacrine
- Administered four times a day
- Side effects include abnormal liver function, nausea, vomiting, diarrhea, abdominal pain, indigestion, and skin rash
- Very rarely prescribed because of side effects, including possible liver damage

Donepezil
- Administered once a day at bedtime
- Comes in tablet form
- Few serious side effects; most common are mild diarrhea, nausea, vomiting, insomnia, fatigue, and weight loss, which usually only last one to three weeks

Rivastigmine
- Available in liquid or capsule form
- In tests, helped slightly more than half of the people who took it
- Side effects include nausea, vomiting, loss of appetite, fatigue, and weight loss; in most cases, the side effects are temporary

Galantamine
- Comes in capsule form
- Derived from daffodil bulbs
- Possible side effects include nausea, vomiting, diarrhea, and weight loss

The newest drug approved for the treatment of Alzheimer's, galantamine, is derived from daffodil bulbs.

Various Methods of Coping

To complement drug therapy, Alzheimer's patients are taught a variety of methods of coping with the early stages of their illness.

Jack Weber, 78, of Lawrenceville, New Jersey, also attends the support group that Allen Scott attends. He has learned a number of techniques to aid his failing memory. At large family gatherings, he will jot down notes on a card so that he can say grace at the table. Before visits to his in-laws, he asks his wife to review everyone's names, which he writes on a sheet of paper and keeps in his pocket. He keeps a small notebook and pen in his breast pocket at all times to make notes to himself.[6]

Scott takes a similar approach. He still drives his van, but he has taught himself to stop at gas stations and ask for directions whenever he gets disoriented. (Even so, he occasionally drives for miles out of his way before realizing that he is lost.)[7]

There are many such tricks Alzheimer's patients can use to keep themselves functioning as independently as possible in the early stage of the disease. Other examples are labeling cupboards and drawers with words or pictures that describe the contents and having a friend or relative call with reminders of meal times, appointments, or times to take medication. A collection of snapshots of people the patient sees regularly, labeled with their names and what they do, can help the patient cope.[8]

Treating Behavioral Symptoms

In addition to the cognitive symptoms of Alzheimer's, there are sometimes behavioral symptoms—changes in the way the patient acts. Some of these changes in behavior can endanger the patient or the people caring for him or her. Among the most common are agitation, aggression, combativeness, suspiciousness, paranoia, delusions, hallucinations, insomnia, and wandering.[9]

These changes in behavior are not always caused directly by Alzheimer's. Sometimes, they are caused by other problems that are treatable, but the Alzheimer's patient is not able to communicate these symptoms to anyone.

For example, the patient might be experiencing physical discomfort from a skin rash or sore, might be suffering from side effects from medication, could have an infection, might be malnourished or dehydrated, or could be losing his or her sight or hearing. In those cases, finding and treating the problem may put a stop to the problem behavior.

There are other methods to deal with changes in behavior. One of the most important steps to be taken is to educate the family, or others responsible for caring for the patient, on what to expect as the disease progresses. That way, they can make a long-term plan and will know what they can do to make the patient as calm and comfortable as possible.

Among the things caregivers can do to deal with difficult behavior is to modify the patient's environment. Lighting, color, and noise can all affect behavior. For example, dim lighting makes some Alzheimer's patients uneasy, while loud, erratic noise can cause confusion and frustration. Making sure that familiar personal possessions are kept visible may also make the patient feel more comfortable and calm.[10]

Finally, organizing a patient's time creates a routine that helps the patient not only remember what he or she needs to do next, but to feel much more relaxed about doing it. A routine helps patients feel more independent and useful. Dressing, cooking, bathing, cleaning, and doing laundry can all help focus the Alzheimer's patient's attention and interest, as can singing, playing a musical instrument, painting, walking, playing with a pet, or reading.[11]

Additional Drugs

If these techniques do not help, there are several drugs that are sometimes prescribed to treat behavioral symptoms. (The four drugs mentioned earlier—tacrine, donepezil, rivastigmine, and galantamine—may help with behavioral symptoms because they improve thinking and reasoning powers, but they are not really intended for that purpose.) The type of drug that may be prescribed depends on the type of behavior that is causing concern.

For patients who are experiencing anxiety, tranquilizers called benzodiazepines (of which Valium® is the best-known example) may be prescribed. Patients suffering from depression are often prescribed antidepressants such as fluoxetine (also known as Prozac®). Insomnia is a common problem among Alzheimer's patients, so drugs that can help bring on sleep are sometimes prescribed. There are many different types of these. For patients suffering from hallucinations or suspiciousness, drugs called antipsychotics may be prescribed. Finally, to combat aggressive behavior, beta-blockers and anti-convulsants may be prescribed.[12]

While these medications may help prevent problem behavior, they must be carefully monitored. It is important to be sure that the medication is actually making a difference and it is also important to watch for possible side-effects and interactions among the various drugs being taken.

For instance, antidepressants can cause drowsiness; antianxiety and sleep medications can add to the confusion the patient is already feeling; antipsychotics sometimes bring on stiff muscles; beta-blockers can lower blood pressure and slow the heart; and anticonvulsants may cause dizziness, to name just a few possibilities.[13]

Alternative Treatments

As is true of other diseases that cannot yet be adequately treated by conventional medicine, a number of alternative treatments for Alzheimer's disease have been suggested. In most cases, there is insufficient scientific evidence to say whether these treatments help. . . or even if they are safe.

Some of the most common alternative treatments people try include Vitamin E, gingko biloba, Huperzine A, Coenzyme Q10, and phosphatidyl serine.

In one study, individuals who took Vitamin E or a drug called selegiline took longer to reach more advanced stages of Alzheimer's disease than those who took a placebo (a substance that has no medical effect on a patient).[14] It did not seem to matter whether they took Vitamin E or selegiline, and taking both did not seem to enhance the effect.

More research remains to be done on Vitamin E because the researchers are not certain if the effect they observed was due to some beneficial effect of Vitamin E on the brain specifically, or just on the overall health of the people involved.[15] Nevertheless, many Alzheimer's patients do take a Vitamin E supplement daily.

Another supplement many people with Alzheimer's (and other memory problems) take is gingko biloba. This plant extract was found in one study to have a positive effect on people with Alzheimer's. The study, led by Pierre L. Le Bars of the New York Institute for Medical Research, found modest improvements in cognition, activities of daily living (such as eating and dressing), and social behavior.[16]

Gingko biloba has been used for centuries in traditional Chinese herbal medicine and, in Europe and some Asian countries, is regularly used to treat a number of symptoms, including dizziness, memory impairment, inflammation, and reduced circulation. In Germany, gingko extracts are an approved treatment for Alzheimer's disease.

However, reported benefits of gingko biloba are small and there is some concern that daily use may cause side effects such as excessive bleeding, particularly when combined with daily use of aspirin.[17]

Huperzine A, which is extracted from moss, is another traditional Chinese medicine. Research has found that it works in the same manner (and just as well) as donepezil, rivastigmine, tacrine, and galantamine. Unfortunately, because it is unregulated and there are therefore no guarantees as to its potency or purity, it is considered somewhat dangerous; an overdose could be disastrous.[18]

Coenzyme Q10, also known as ubiquinone, occurs naturally in the body. It has not been studied for its effectiveness in treating Alzheimer's. A synthetic version, called idebenone, was tested, but with no favorable results. There is no research to say how much Coenzyme Q10 can be safely taken, much less whether it actually helps Alzheimer's patients.

Finally, phosphatidyl serine is another naturally occurring compound that was studied as a treatment for Alzheimer's disease several years ago but did not improve cognitive abilities. Some small, inconclusive studies have shown that people without Alzheimer's can think and reason better when they take phosphatidyl serine.[19]

In the end, the unhappy truth is that there are currently no truly effective treatments for Alzheimer's. The best that a patient can hope for is to buy a little more time before the worst effects of the disease take hold—and then to have caregivers who will do their best to make him or her as comfortable as possible.

Enhancing Dignity and Quality of Life

To that end, new approaches are now being tried to increase the quality of life of people with Alzheimer's disease.

For instance, at the St. Elizabeth Center in downtown Waco, Texas, the fourth floor has been turned into an indoor park, complete with a street lamp, garden, and park benches. The goal of the "Crossroads" floor is to provide the fifty-two residents with advanced Alzheimer's disease with an active, familiar environment that helps to stimulate pleasant personal memories.

The floor is divided into sections depicting different aspects of life. There is a restaurant decorated with an antique radio, a washboard, and old poster advertisements. Future plans include a general store, barber shop, gym, chapel, theater, and an ice cream parlor.

Daily activities are planned to provide patients with a sense of normality. Each day, a beautician fixes the residents' hair and staff members lead exercise classes, cooking sessions, worship services, and sing-alongs.

"The goal is introducing choices for the residents, allowing them freedom to participate in whatever they're capable of," says Doug Wuenschel, president and chief executive officer of Christus the Regis/St. Elizabeth Centers. "The goal is to increase the quality of life and help them maintain their self-respect and dignity—to keep them humanized."[20]

Newly designed residential facilities for Alzheimer's are springing up all over, thanks to calls from specialists like Elizabeth Brawley, author of *Designing for Alzheimer's Disease*, for lots of light to eliminate frightening shadows and help reduce depression. Light is especially important late in the afternoon and early in the evening; that's when something called "sundowning" occurs in many Alzheimer's patients. They suffer increased confusion, anxiety, agitation, and disorientation beginning at dusk and continuing throughout the night.

Alzheimer's patients also tend to wander, and new facilities are being designed that actually permit a certain amount of wandering, featuring enclosed gardens with circular paths. A study by the University of Pittsburgh and Carnegie Mellon University of a senior center with garden walkways found that residents remained just as mobile at the end of 18 months as they were at the beginning, whereas in an ordinary nursing home, they were 25 percent less mobile at the end of that time.

Smaller, more home-like settings for Alzheimer's patients to live in seem to help, as well. Kitchens and laundry rooms allow them to wash dishes and fold clothing—which may not sound very exciting, but patients who have lost the ability to do many other things appreciate having tasks that they can still perform. "It not only keeps them busy, it gives them a sense of accomplishment and dignity," says Uriel Clohen of the University of Wisconsin-Milwaukee's Institute on Aging and Environment.

Simple one-on-one interactions with other people, whether in a conversation or just clipping coupons, can calm Alzheimer's patients, cutting the number of disruptive verbal outbursts in half. Music, aquariums, aromatherapy— researchers are trying many new ways to keep Alzheimer's patients engaged and interested in life.

As Dr. David Bennett, director of the Alzheimer's disease Center at Chicago's Rush-Presbyterian-St. Luke's Medical Center, says, "Even though they can't do what they used to do, that doesn't mean they can't enjoy life at the moment."[21]

6

Social Implications of Alzheimer's Disease

All diseases take a toll on society. Even the common cold has a social cost—lost productivity, lost wages, days missed from school.

A disease's toll is also felt on a smaller social scale, in families and groups of friends, all of whom are affected by the illness of a single person.

Alzheimer's, in many ways, is hardest on the families and friends of the person with the disease. While in the early stages the patient is keenly aware of the problems he or she is having, eventually the disease robs him or her of that awareness. The people who know and love the patient, however, are constantly aware that the person they knew is gone for good, even though he or she is still physically present. Loved ones must also usually bear the physical, emotional, and financial cost of caring for the Alzheimer's patient, at least until the final stages of the disease, when many patients end up in a hospital or other institution.

In one national survey, 19 million Americans said they had a family member with Alzheimer's disease, and 37 million said they knew someone with the disease—just one indication of the emotional toll Alzheimer's exacts.[1]

Financial Impact

The financial impact of Alzheimer's is felt on both an individual and national scale. On the national scale, the Alzheimer's Association estimates the disease costs the United States at least $100 billion a year. The cost to business is estimated at more than $33 billion—$26 billion due to lost productivity of people who are caring for family members with Alzheimer's and the rest going to cover the business share of the costs of health and long-term care.[2]

Much of the total financial cost of Alzheimer's is borne by the family and friends of Alzheimer's patients. More than seven out of ten people with Alzheimer's disease live at home, and although three-quarters of the home care patients require is provided by family and friends, the rest of it has to be paid for, at an average cost of $12,500 per year.[3]

Eventually, most Alzheimer's patients end up in nursing homes, where half of all residents suffer from Alzheimer's or a related disorder. The average cost for nursing home care across the United States is $42,000 per year; it can be more than $70,000 a year in some parts of the country.[4]

Add it all up and the average lifetime cost of care is $174,000 per Alzheimer's patient. And neither Medicare nor most private health insurance covers the long-term care required.[5]

Research into the disease is also expensive. The federal government alone estimates it spent $466 million on Alzheimer's disease research in 2000.[6]

The money adds up, but the social implications of Alzheimer's go far beyond the financial cost. The real burden is borne by family and friends who lose loved ones to the disease.

A Devastated Family

Carolyn Ives of Roswell, New Mexico, lost her husband, Harry, to Alzheimer's in October of 1998. They had been married for more than 50 years, but as the disease progressed, she could no longer communicate with him. She would try to talk to him, but what he would say would not make sense. He would look at her expectantly but she would not know what to say to him. "You can't talk to him," she says. "You are no longer in the same world as the person."

Caring for such a person is difficult. Dolly Vowell, also of Roswell, eventually had to put her husband, Jeff, in a nursing home. "I know at the time the doctors told me my husband had Alzheimer's I had no idea what I was in for," she says. "Nothing prepared me for what happened. It is like a regression to the womb. They just go back and forget everything."

When her husband was first diagnosed, she used to try to go to quilting meetings, setting out breakfast and lunch for her husband and leaving a note saying where she was and when she would be back. But one day she returned and her husband asked her where she had been; he had forgotten how to read.

Eventually, he became very suspicious, hiding things around the house, then losing them and blaming other people for taking them.

Dolly took care of her husband for ten years before putting him in the nursing home. The constant care took so much out of her that she fell into a severe depression. "You actually have to live with it to understand what it is all about," she says.

Jim Markl, former chair of the Alzheimer's Support Group of Roswell, says that taking care of an Alzheimer's patient is more than a full day's work. "Every day is like 36 hours instead of 24," he says. His sister suffered from Alzheimer's and would sometimes get up in the middle of the night and pack her bags for California. He took her picture to the Roswell Police Department, just in case she wandered off.[7]

Affects Family in Different Ways

When someone in the family has Alzheimer's, it affects everyone in the family in different ways.

If the person is married, his or her spouse probably suffers the most. Alzheimer's changes the relationship between the two partners. The healthy spouse may have to take on new and unfamiliar tasks, learning to balance a checkbook for the first time, for instance, or learning to cook. Routines change. The level of companionship changes, as the spouse with Alzheimer's begins to withdraw into his or her own world. It becomes harder to enjoy a normal social life. Finances may suffer. And, of course, all plans for the future are changed to reflect the stark reality that the person with Alzheimer's is going to continue to deteriorate.

Debbie White of Arlington, Virginia, is only 44. Her husband, Eddie, is 66, and was diagnosed with Alzheimer's in 1996.

Today, she holds down a full-time job while continuing to care for her husband. When she goes off to work, he goes to an adult day-care facility, because he cannot be left alone anymore. In the evening, she cares for him the same way she would a small child—hiding dangerous items, locking him into the bedroom at night because he once wandered miles away in his bathrobe, and leaving appliances unplugged because he recently turned on the stove when things were piled on top.

"I have got to be in the same room as him," Mrs. White says. "He doesn't know his surroundings as well as he used to."

She keeps the dozen pills her husband takes every day locked up in a suitcase-sized plastic box and makes sure he takes them when he is supposed to. He gets irritable between 4 and 7 p.m. and demands to go home, even though he is already there.

Mrs. White knows that caring for her husband could go on for decades. "People say to me, you're only 44! This is going to be your life?" she says. "But I hope to keep him home. Eventually, I know he might have to go to a nursing home, but they'll have to take him out of here with me kicking and screaming."[8]

It is not surprising that the spouses of people with Alzheimer's who are also caregivers are at a high risk of depression.[9] The slow, irrevocable decline brought on by Alzheimer's results in the living spouse essentially mourning the death of someone they may have spent half a century with—while that person's body is still alive.[10]

Children Affected, Too

In addition to, or instead of, the spouse, many caregivers for Alzheimer's patients are adult children of the patient. It is obviously stressful for any child to suddenly be thrust into the position of having to care for his or her father or mother. It can be even more stressful when the other parent is looking after most of the care, because then the child worries about both parents.

One common emotion felt by adult children is guilt, because they have often moved away from home and are not in a position to help with the care as much as they feel they should.[11]

Their children, the grandchildren of the person with Alzheimer's, are also affected. How a child reacts to Alzheimer's disease depends on the child, but common reactions include:

- Fear that the disease is contagious and they or their parents may catch it (they will not);

Children can also be affected when a family member has Alzheimer's disease. They may feel that they did something that caused the illness, they may think that it is contagious and that their parents may catch it, or they may feel fear, resentment, and anxiety.

- Guilt—a feeling they somehow did or thought something that caused the illness (they did not);

- Resentment, because their parents are caring for the Alzheimer's patient instead of being there for them;

- Anxiety or embarrassment because the Alzheimer's patient is acting strangely, which may make them reluctant to ask friends over; or

- Anger, because they have to take on more responsibilities because everyone else is busy looking after the Alzheimer's patient.

Some of these emotions can lead to behavioral problems like bed-wetting, problems in school, or depression, adding more stress to an already stressed-out family.[12]

Caregivers Must Watch Own Health

Of course, guilt, resentment, and anger are not limited to children. Adult caregivers feel these emotions, too, and they can lead to adult behavioral problems like an inability to perform well at work or increased use of alcohol or drugs. For that reason, it is important that caregivers monitor their own physical and emotional health closely.

One very useful method is the support group. Support groups are groups of caregivers, family, friends, and others affected by Alzheimer's disease who gather to discuss issues related to the disease and help each other to deal with the difficulties it raises. Many communities have support groups for the caregivers of Alzheimer's patients, often sponsored by the Alzheimer's Association.

Other caregivers prefer to get their support from family, friends, or their church. The important thing is that caregivers find some way to deal with the ongoing stress, which may last for many years, of looking after an Alzheimer's patient.[13]

Financially, emotionally, and physically, Alzheimer's takes its toll on everyone who comes into contact with it.

7
Preventing Alzheimer's Disease

Brendan Shanahan plays left wing with the Detroit Red Wings of the National Hockey League (NHL). Originally from Toronto, Brendan became fascinated with hockey at an early age, like many other Canadian kids—and his father, Donal, shared his passion, even though he had never played hockey himself.

"My father was always there for me, driving me to games religiously and even tying my skates. He never coached me in hockey but my father's lessons went beyond the game. To win, you had to earn it, and he would get very upset if I showed poor sportsmanship. I had to play fair before anything else, those were the rules," Brendan recalls.

But when Brendan was 14, his father's behavior began to change. He showed signs of confusion, and the confusion got worse. A year later, Brendan's father, just 52 years old, was diagnosed with Alzheimer's disease, leaving Brendan frustrated and impatient. "I didn't know what was happening and couldn't understand. I never heard of Alzheimer's until my dad was diagnosed with it—even then, the whole thing was very foreign to me."

His father was no longer confident driving him to games. Sometimes he would get lost; sometimes he could not remember where to insert the car keys. The last time Brendan's father drove a car was to take Brendan to the licensing bureau to get his own driver's license.

By the time Brendan was drafted into the NHL at 18, his father could not really understand what was happening. He never saw Brendan play in the NHL. He died when Brendan was 21 and playing for the New Jersey Devils.

Brendan would have given anything for a way to prevent Alzheimer's. "Alzheimer's can be harder on the family than the person suffering from it," he says. "My father was the backbone of our family and it was very difficult to see, let alone accept what was happening to him."

Today, Brendan continues to support Alzheimer's research and helps to raise money for the cause. "Our parents deserve to age gracefully," he says. "Alzheimer's is a long, slow and sad goodbye that no one needs to go through."[1]

Uncertainty Hampers Prevention

Because the cause of Alzheimer's is still uncertain, it is not known how the disease can be prevented. However, a number of factors have been identified that seem to make it more likely that an individual will develop Alzheimer's. Some of these factors are preventable. . . and some are not.

Most cases of Alzheimer's are probably brought on by a combination of factors, but early-onset Alzheimer's (Alzheimer's which occurs before age 65) is often brought on by damage to specific genes.

Scientists have identified three mutations that are so damaging that inheriting any one of them almost guarantees that a person will develop Alzheimer's sometime between the ages of 30 and 60. Most people who may have one of these mutations are already aware of the risk, because they will usually have seen their parents or other close relatives develop Alzheimer's at an early age.

The three early-onset Alzheimer's genes that have been identified are called APP, Chromosome 21; Presenilin-1, Chromosome 14; and Presenilin-2, Chromosome 1.

APP, Chromosome 21 affects the body's production of beta amyloid—the protein that forms the plaques on Alzheimer's patients' brain cells. Presenilin-1 and Presenilin-2 also affect production of this protein. However, each of these mutations accounts for only a small percentage of Alzheimer's cases. The APP mutation is thought to account for less than one percent; in people with this mutation, the symptoms first occur between the ages of 45 and 65. The Presenilin-1 mutation is thought to account for perhaps 4 percent of cases, with onset of symptoms between ages 28 and 50, and the Presenilin-2 mutation is thought to account for another one percent of cases, with onset of symptoms between the ages of 40 and 50.[2]

Another mutation appears to increase the risk of Alzheimer's in other people who develop the disease later in life. A mutation in a gene called ApoE4, Chromosome 19, which tells the body to produce a common lipoprotein that is also known to be a risk factor for heart disease, appears in 65 percent of Alzheimer's patients. However, many other people who inherit this mutated gene do not develop Alzheimer's at all, even in their 90s, which indicates that while it may increase the risk of the disease, it does not directly cause it.[3]

Knowing some of the genes whose mutation may trigger Alzheimer's helps scientists looking for new drugs to treat the disease, but does not provide individuals with anything they can do to prevent the disease. You either have one of these mutated genes, or you do not.

There are probably many other genes involved in increasing the risk of Alzheimer's. Studies indicate that people who have one parent stricken with the disease are three times more likely to develop Alzheimer's themselves than people whose parents did not have the disease. People whose parents were both affected are five times more likely to contract the disease.[4]

However, scientists think that these genes, while still unidentified, probably do not directly cause the disease. Instead, they simply make the people with the genes more susceptible to something in their environment that triggers Alzheimer's.

Studies with identical twins who share the same genetic makeup make that clear. Sally Luxon and Diane Schuller are 63-year-old identical twins from Ohio. Diane looks younger than her age and enjoys traveling with her husband and spending time with her children and her grandchildren. Her sister, Sally, suffers from advanced Alzheimer's, has not spoken since 1993, has not walked since 1994, and does not recognize family members—including Diane. "You just hold her hand," Diane says, "and hope that when you give her a hug and kiss, somewhere deep down she knows you're there."[5]

So, what are some of the environmental factors that can help bring on Alzheimer's in some people?

One seems to be head trauma. Researchers know from autopsy studies that people who have suffered head trauma also suffer an acute buildup of beta amyloid plaques. In one five-year study involving 2,000 elderly people in New York, Dr. Richard Mayeux of Columbia University found that those who had been knocked unconscious as adults developed Alzheimer's at a rate three times greater than those who had not.[6]

Research also indicates that people with less education suffer higher rates of Alzheimer's. In one recent survey conducted by scientists at Indiana University, African Americans with rural backgrounds and less than seven years of schooling suffered 6.5 times more Alzheimer's than better-educated city-dwellers.[7]

Scientists are not sure, though, if it is the lack of education that leads to Alzheimer's, or if lack of education is an indication of other forms of deprivation in childhood that increase the risk of developing the disease.

Another study that indicates a poor environment in childhood leads to greater risk of Alzheimer's later in life is one that found that people from large families have a greater risk of Alzheimer's disease than people from smaller families. In the study of 770 people aged 60 and older conducted by Victoria Moceri of the University of Washington, the risk of developing Alzheimer's increased by 8 percent for each additional sibling in the family. The reason, Moceri hypothesizes, is that children in larger families are more likely to suffer from a poor-quality childhood environment, which "could prevent the brain from reaching a complete level of maturation. The effects of impaired development could produce a brain that is normal, but functions less efficiently." The effects would not be noticed until they were aggravated by the aging process.[8]

Specific toxins in the environment have also been implicated in a greater risk for Alzheimer's. Research led by Elisabeth Koss of Case Western Reserve University and University Hospitals of Cleveland, Ohio, found that people who work on jobs with high levels of lead exposure are up to 3.4 times more likely to develop Alzheimer's disease. Activities that expose workers to lead include smelting or casting lead, removing lead coatings (such as old paints), heating, machining or spraying lead products, and making lead products (which include automobile batteries, ammunition, lead pipe, electronic components, and some paints and inks).[9]

Exercise Helps

Several studies have indicated that one way to reduce the risk of contracting Alzheimer's disease in old age is to keep both one's brain and body active.

A thirty-five-year study of 5,000 Seattle residents has found that people who stay physically fit are more likely to remain

Aluminum and Alzheimer's

In the 1960s, scientists experimented with injecting rats with aluminum compounds; they found this led to more neurofibrillary tangles in the rats' brains—tangles similar to those that appear in Alzheimer's patients.

From that result, many people came to believe that aluminum might be an environmental risk factor for Alzheimer's. Some went so far as to get rid of aluminum pots and pans.

Other studies have indicated that people who live in areas with low levels of aluminum in their drinking water have less chance of developing Alzheimer's disease than those who live where levels of aluminum in the drinking water are higher.[10]

On the other hand, the same study that indicated lead exposure put workers at higher risk of Alzheimer's also looked at exposure to aluminum, copper, iron, mercury, zinc, and solvents (paint thinners, for instance)—and found a link only to lead exposure.

The researchers believe that the concern over the other metals and solvents may have been due to the unrecognized effect of lead.[11]

At the moment, the jury is out on the hazards of aluminum exposure. Future studies should clarify the risks further.

mentally fit. Another study has demonstrated that older people who start walking regularly can improve cognitive skills such as the ability to switch quickly from one mental task to another.[12]

Several studies have indicated that mental exercise is important, too. For example, a study conducted by Robert Friedland, a neurologist at Case Western Reserve University School of Medicine and University Hospitals of Cleveland, found that people who were not very active outside of work were more than three times more likely to develop Alzheimer's disease than people who were active outside of work. The type of activity didn't seem to matter: playing a musical instrument, gardening, exercising, or even playing board games all seemed

A thirty-five-year study of 5,000 Seattle residents has found that people who stay physically fit are more likely to remain mentally fit.

to help. (Watching television, attending church and ordinary social activities did not.)[13]

"Intellectual activity is like weight training for brain neurons," says Dr. Friedland. "The brain is an organ for learning. It is a case of 'use it or lose it.'"[14]

Supplements May Help

There may be more direct approaches to preventing Alzheimer's, according to other research. For instance, it

Workouts for the Brain[18]

Here are some examples of intellectual activities that may help reduce the risk of developing Alzheimer's later in life:

- Reading
- Constructing jigsaw puzzles
- Working crossword puzzles
- Playing a musical instrument
- Working on various crafts
- Painting, drawing, or performing other artwork
- Doing woodworking projects
- Writing letters
- Playing card games
- Engaging in board games such as checkers, chess, Monopoly, and Scrabble
- Doing home repairs
- Knitting or needlework

appears that the beta amyloid plaques that build up in the brain of Alzheimer's patients promote oxidation, a form of chemical damage that kills brain cells. Research suggests that antioxidants such as Vitamin E may help prevent that damage. Some studies have found that a high blood level of Vitamin E translates to good cognitive function and a low risk of Alzheimer's in humans.[15]

Another way that plaques damage brain cells is by triggering inflammation. Studies have suggested that people who take anti-inflammatory drugs, including ordinary aspirin, may have a reduced risk of Alzheimer's.[16]

Research also suggests that people suffering from even a slight deficiency of Vitamin B-12 and folic acid may be at greater risk of Alzheimer's.[17]

Some of the evidence for that comes from one of the major studies currently underway into Alzheimer's, involving 678 nuns from the School Sisters of Notre Dame, who have agreed to donate their brains to research.[19] Autopsies of the nuns whose brains show signs of Alzheimer's have shown that they have lower blood levels of folic acid than those with normal brains; living nuns with the highest levels of folic acid have shown the least cognitive decline.[20]

Researchers suspect that the reason B-12 and folic acid deficiency may contribute to Alzheimer's is that such a deficiency boosts a blood compound called homocysteine. Another recent study has linked high homocysteine levels to increased risk of Alzheimer's.

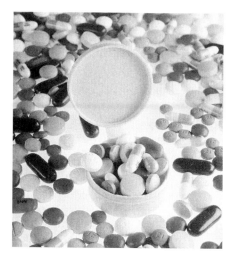

Studies have suggested that antioxidants such as Vitamin E, anti-inflammatory drugs such as aspirin, and supplements of Vitamin B-12 and folic acid could help reduce the risk of Alzheimer's disease.

Because many older people do not secrete enough stomach acid to extract and absorb vitamin B-12 from their food, they are at particular risk of developing this deficiency—a deficiency that can be easily counteracted by taking B-12 and folic acid supplements or eating foods rich in these substances.[21] Vitamin B-12, for instance, is found in most animal-based foods, including fish, milk and milk products, eggs, meat, and poultry. Leafy greens such as spinach, turnip greens, dry beans and peas, grain products, and some fruits and vegetables are rich food sources of folic acid.

Hormone Replacement

Women may develop Alzheimer's more often than men of the same age, which could be due to the drop in levels of the female hormone estrogen in women past menopause. Estrogen fights oxidation and inflammation, and may boost the level of the brain chemical acetylcholine (the same chemical the drugs currently approved to fight Alzheimer's boost). Older men actually have higher levels of estrogen than older women, because their bodies convert some of the male hormone testosterone to estrogen.[22]

A 1996 study of 1,300 elderly women conducted by Dr. Richard Mayeux of Columbia University found that those who underwent estrogen replacement therapy after menopause reduced their Alzheimer's risk by half.[23] However, the benefit only appears to apply to women who have not yet contracted the disease. A study by neuroscientist Ruth A. Mulnard from the University of California at Irvine found that estrogen did nothing to improve the mental functioning of 120 older women with mild to moderate Alzheimer's. (However, all 120 women had undergone hysterectomies [removal of the uterus]; further studies are needed to see if estrogen replacement therapy might benefit women with Alzheimer's whose uteruses are intact.)[24]

If all of these suggestions as to how the risk of Alzheimer's might be reduced sound a bit "iffy," they are; we are in the midst of a huge wave of Alzheimer's-related research, and as with all scientific research, some studies seem to contradict other studies.

As research continues, better and more effective ways to prevent Alzheimer's disease will surely be discovered.

8

Research and the Future

Rip Tuttle, 55, of Eden Prairie, Minnesota, is an ex-Marine and former business manager who used to handle multi-million-dollar budgets. He used to lead Boy Scouts and coach baseball, softball, football, and soccer. Now he needs help with basic activities such as eating and dressing.

"What gets me is I used to do big reports and now I can't remember. . . can't remember. . . "

His wife, Linda, has to finish the sentence for him. "Words?" she says.

"Yeah, words."

Linda, 48, helps Rip stay engaged with church, friends, and family. She tries to calm him and reassure him. "Every day is a series of small struggles—staying calm when Rip becomes so angry that he throws things because he can't dress himself, or the words don't come out right," she says. "Today is good. Yesterday was bad."

Rip takes Aricept®, one of the four drugs approved to treat Alzheimer's in the United States. He takes aspirin and Vitamin E. He is doing everything he can, based on the current level of knowledge about Alzheimer's—but it is not enough.

"There has been gradual loss," Linda says. "Mixed in with our joy at still having each other, we're in a continual state of grief over the small losses here and there."

There is little hope that current research will make much of a difference to the course of the disease in the case of Rip Tuttle and other patients who already have Alzheimer's, but there is hope for the future.

"Five years? That's too soon," says Alzheimer's researcher Hugh Hendrie. "Ten years? Fifteen? Oh, it's an exciting time in this field. We're learning so much. I think we can at least delay the onset and progression of Alzheimer's."

Or, as Rip Tuttle told his 23-year-old son Chris, "This is my problem, but it won't be yours. They'll have a pill."[1]

Improved Diagnosis

When and if a pill is developed, early diagnosis of Alzheimer's is likely to be very important for successful treatment of the disease, particularly if the pill does not cure the disease but can slow or halt its progression. If that is the case, the ideal situation would be to be able to diagnose the disease before symptoms appear.

A method of early diagnosis might also help researchers monitor the progression of the disease in people undergoing experimental treatments, which would make the development of new treatments more efficient. It might also make existing drugs and preventative treatments such as Vitamin E and anti-inflammatory drugs more effective.

Research at the University of Pennsylvania School of Medicine points the way to just such a method of diagnosis and monitoring. A team led by Virginia M. Y. Lee has created a molecule called BSB that binds to beta amyloid plaques. Just as important, it is able to penetrate the blood-brain barrier, a

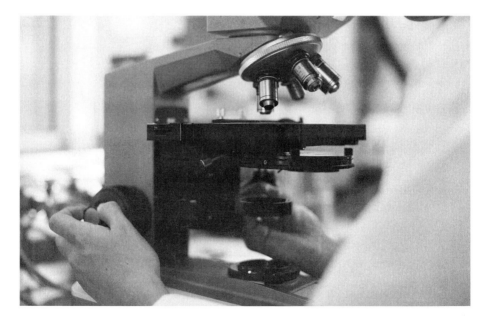

A method of early diagnosis could help researchers monitor the progression of the disease, which would make the development of new treatments more effective.

natural barrier that protects the brain from toxins, bacteria, and viruses in the blood.

When injected into mice that have been genetically modified to develop plaques like those characteristic of Alzheimer's disease, BSB travels to the brain and attaches itself to the plaques, remaining there for at least 18 hours. Attaching a radioactive marker to the BSB molecule should make it possible to see plaques using X-rays and other medical imaging equipment.

If BSB can be made to work in humans, it could make it possible to diagnose Alzheimer's in living brains in the early stages of the disease.

"This tool could help clinicians peer into a person's brain and monitor amyloid levels in response to treatment," says Marcelle Morrison-Bogorad, Associate Director of Neuroscience and Neuropsychology of Aging at the National Institute on Aging in Bethesda, Maryland. "We definitely need something like this to advance the diagnosis and treatment of dementia."

Another tool that may help with the early diagnosis of Alzheimer's is structural magnetic resonance imaging (MRI). According to research done by Marilyn Albert and colleagues of Massachusetts General Hospital and Harvard Medical School, MRI scans can be used to diagnose Alzheimer's before symptoms appear by measuring the size of regions of the brain that are affected by Alzheimer's. (Because Alzheimer's leads to the death of brain cells, affected regions shrink.) Further research is needed to refine the technique to the point where it will be useful on a regular basis.

"Effective treatments for Alzheimer's disease are likely to be ready over the next decade or so," says Albert. "In the not-too-distant future, we may be able to use MRI, in combination with other measures, to identify people at highest risk who can be effectively treated as these new therapies come along."[2]

Hopes for a Treatment

Albert's prediction that effective treatments for Alzheimer's will become available within the next ten years or so is widely shared by other researchers.

The most exciting recent development has been research that raises the tantalizing possibility of a vaccine for Alzheimer's, one that would not only prevent the development of the disease, but might help to treat it.

In 1999, a team of researchers led by Dale Schenk at Elan Corporation in San Francisco reported in the journal *Nature* that they had injected mice that had been genetically modified to develop beta amyloid plaques with amyloid combined with substances that excite the immune system. The goal was to train the mice's immune systems to attack amyloid, in the hope that this would prevent amyloid plaques from forming.

When their brains were dissected a year later, the mice who had received the injection showed few or no plaques, while mice that had not been vaccinated had extensive plaques.

Next, the researchers injected twenty-four 1-year-old mice who had already developed plaques with the vaccine, while twenty-four similar mice did not receive the vaccine.

"We saw that it completely stopped the further progression of the disease," Schenk says. "It looks like it might have actually diminished the plaques."[3]

At the World Alzheimer's Congress 2000, held in Washington, D.C., in July, 2000, this research dominated discussion. At that conference, Schenk reported that vaccinated guinea pigs, rabbits, monkeys, and other animals showed no indications of toxic reactions to the vaccine. A Phase I clinical trial of the vaccine, designed to see if it is safe to use in humans, also produced encouraging results, with twenty-four patients who received a single dose of the vaccine showing no ill effects.[4]

Other researchers reported studies that have duplicated the Elan results. Christopher Janus and colleagues at the University of Toronto compared the performance of vaccinated and non-vaccinated mice in what is called the Morris water maze, a standard memory test in which animals are supposed to learn the location of a submerged platform in a water bath. They found that weeks after Alzheimer's-like memory problems appeared in the non-treated mice, treated mice performed as well as mice that had not been engineered to develop amyloid plaques.

In a similar study, David Morgan and his colleagues at the University of South Florida in Tampa modified the water maze so they could count how many wrong turns the mice took while searching for the hidden platform. First, they trained the mice to find the platform, then waited 30 minutes and let them try again. Mice with amyloid plaques could not find the platform, but vaccinated mice remembered the location almost perfectly, just as well as regular mice.

Those results excited researchers. "The fact that mice are helped behaviorally gives a big boost to the discussion of the potential utility of this technique in humans," says Stephen DeKosky, a neurologist at the University of Pittsburgh.[5]

At the time this book was being written, a British trial of the vaccine on humans was being carried out, with volunteers receiving a dose every two months for a year. Scientists were anxiously awaiting the results.[6]

Elan Corporation, the pharmaceutical company that initiated the research into an amyloid vaccine, hopes to begin conducting trials that determine its effectiveness in humans late in 2001. If it is effective, it will be at least a year after that before the company applies to the Food and Drug Administration for a license to market the vaccine, and months after that before it might be available to the public.[7]

A New Drug

While the amyloid vaccine is exciting, other ways of treating Alzheimer's are also being researched. In the shorter term, memantine, a drug already being used in Germany, shows promise of being able to significantly slow the progression of Alzheimer's in patients during the moderately severe stage of the disease.

How Glowing Jellyfish Help Alzheimer's Research

A gene that normally makes jellyfish glow green is helping Alzheimer's researchers understand how the neurofibrillary tangles form in the brains of people suffering from the disease.

When researchers put the jellyfish gene into brain cells, it lights up the tau protein that normally holds the fibers of the nerve cells together. In people with Alzheimer's disease, tau proteins break away and form tangles that keep the nerve cells from working properly.

Using the jellyfish gene, Professor Simon Lovestone, head of old-age psychiatry at the Institute of Psychiatry in London, England, was able to see how a particular enzyme makes tau come off of the nerve fibers. Even more importantly, he was able to confirm that lithium can block the enzyme, making tau reattach itself properly.

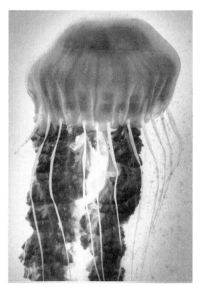

Although still in its early stages, the research made possible by the jellyfish gene could someday lead to new, more effective treatments for Alzheimer's disease.

Unlike the four drugs currently approved in the United States, which boost the brain chemical acetylcholine, memantine makes brain cells less able to respond to another chemical, called glutamate. Oversensitivity to glutamate may damage the brain cells.

The study, conducted by neuropsychiatrist Barry Reisberg of New York University School of Medicine, involved 252 Alzheimer's patients, all of whom had reached the point where they were beginning to lose the ability to dress or bathe themselves. All the patients in the study experienced a decline in mental ability over the 28 weeks of the trial, but those who received memantine experienced a slower decline. The drug also caused few side effects. If the FDA approves the drug, it could be available in the United States within a year or two. Meanwhile, its success will result in research aimed at developing other drugs that take the same approach.[8]

Rebuilding Brain Cells

A completely different approach to treating Alzheimer's is being taken by a team of scientists at the University of California, San Diego, led by Mark H. Tuszynski. Their research focuses on gene therapy: They plan to use a disabled virus that normally causes cancer to introduce nerve-growth factors into the brain that prevent cell death and can coax damaged brain cells back to life.

The technique has stimulated the growth of new brain cells in both rats and rhesus monkeys with no signs of adverse effects. The next step is testing Alzheimer's patients to see if it is safe for humans. This testing began in March of 2001.

The first step in the procedure is taking a sample of skin from the patient. Skin cells contain immature cells called fibroblasts which can be made to multiply in a test tube. While that is occurring, a virus that normally causes leukemia is activated by removing the gene from it that tells it to divide. Then, the genes that tell human cells to make nerve-growth factors are inserted into the virus, instead.

The fibroblasts are modified with the viral mixture, so that they will start turning out nerve growth factors. Then the mixture of viruses and fibroblasts is injected into the brain. Tuszynski thinks that a yearly injection should be enough.

"This is a reliable, efficient and practical way to stimulate nerve cell growth," he says, and unlike current drugs, "would prevent—not patch."

Once the safety of the procedure is established, a larger trial will be held to see if the treatment can slow or halt the progression of Alzheimer's.[9]

Seeking Out the Cause

Meanwhile, new research into the basic causes of Alzheimer's continues. Each piece of the puzzle that is discovered provides other researchers with targets for possible treatments.

For example, in June, 2000, researchers at Merck Research Laboratories in West Point, Pennsylvania, reported that they had discovered the enzyme that turns the naturally occurring

Brain Scan May Provide Early Alzheimer's Diagnosis

In November, 2001, an international research team led by Dr. Daniel H.S. Silverman of the UCLA School of Medicine announced that a type of brain scan called positron emission tomography, or PET, can detect early changes in the brain that indicate a high risk of developing full-blown Alzheimer's disease.

As people develop the disease, the way their brains use nutrients such as sugar changes. The PET scan can detect these changes before any other symptoms develop.

The study looked at 300 people who sought medical help for recent problems with concentration and thinking, or changes in behavior or personality. About 150 received a brain PET scan and were then followed for an average of three years to see if symptoms worsened. Another 150 had the initial scan and also underwent an autopsy when they died.

The vast majority of the people whose brains showed early metabolic changes did indeed develop a severe dementia, usually Alzheimer's disease. Those whose PET scans did not reveal the metabolic changes were unlikely to lose additional brain function during the three years.

The researchers believe the PET scan can help patients by allowing doctors to detect Alzheimer's in its early stages, when aggressive treatment can help stave off symptoms. It can also help relieve the fear of Alzheimer's for people with normal scan results.[11]

amyloid protein into the sticky beta amyloid protein that forms the plaques on brain cells in Alzheimer's patients.

According to the researchers, this enzyme, which they had been calling gamma secretase, is actually Presenilin-1—an enzyme already linked to early-onset Alzheimer's. A team at Harvard Medical School, working independently, also claimed gamma secretase and Presenilin-1 are one and the same.

Identifying one of the enzymes that cuts amyloid protein into beta amyloid protein is important because it gives drug company researchers a target: They can now attempt to develop drugs that block the action of the enzyme. "This is not just pie-in-the-sky," says Dennis Selkoe, a neurobiologist on the Harvard team. "There is a palpable sense that knowing what gamma secretase is, we should be able to inhibit it."[10]

For Alzheimer's researchers everywhere, this is an exciting time. "We've learned more about Alzheimer's in the past 15 years than in the previous 85," says Dr. Bruce Yankner of Harvard Medical School.

Or, as Dr. Marcelle Morrison-Bogorad puts it, "We've never been at a stage like this, where we have so many leads to follow."

The next few years promise to revolutionize the treatment of Alzheimer's—and, just maybe, eliminate the fear of this deadly mind-thief once and for all.

Q&A

Q. Isn't memory loss a natural part of aging?

A. While it is true that many healthy people find it harder to remember certain kinds of information as they get older, Alzheimer's disease causes more than simple lapses in memory. People with Alzheimer's have trouble communicating, learning, thinking and reasoning to the extent that it interferes with their work and their social and family life. That is not a normal part of aging.

Q. How many people are affected by Alzheimer's disease?

A. One in ten people over 65 and almost half of those over 85 have the disease. Currently, four million Americans suffer from it. It is estimated that the number will jump to 14 million by 2050 unless a cure or treatment is found. As well, 19 million Americans have a family member with Alzheimer's disease, and 37 million know someone with the disease.

Q. Does Alzheimer's disease run in families?

A. The evidence is not clear. It is rare to find a family where several members have been diagnosed with Alzheimer's. It is much more common to find a single family member who develops the disease late in life.

Q. Doesn't Alzheimer's only occur in old people?

A. No. The disease can occur in people in their thirties, forties, and fifties. However, this early-onset form of the disease accounts for less than 10 percent of all reported cases and seems to be inherited.

Q. Can Alzheimer's be cured?

A. No. There is no cure for the disease at this time. The only treatments available are four drugs that work by boosting the production of a brain chemical that helps brain cells communicate. However, these drugs only improve mental ability a small amount—usually equivalent to six months of decline. These drugs are not effective for all patients.

Q. Is Alzheimer's disease fatal?

A. Yes. Because Alzheimer's destroys brain cells, the brain eventually degenerates to the point where it can no longer maintain the functioning of the body. However, because Alzheimer's typically occurs in older adults and may take twenty years to run its course, many Alzheimer's patients die of other ailments before Alzheimer's itself kills them.

Q. Can I get Alzheimer's by drinking out of aluminum cans or by using aluminum pots?

A. No. Most researchers believe there is not enough evidence to consider aluminum a risk factor for Alzheimer's. In addition, you are exposed to much more aluminum from other sources—aluminum is the third most common element found in the Earth's crust, after oxygen and silicon.

Q. Can I get Alzheimer's from drinking diet drinks containing aspartame?

A. No. Several studies have been conducted on aspartame's effect on cognitive function in both animals and humans, and have found no link between aspartame and memory loss.

Alzheimer's Disease Timeline

Ninth century B.C.—Ancient Egyptian records speak of chronic forgetfulness among elderly people.

Approx. A.D. 100—Claudius Galen, a Roman doctor, writes about age-related forgetfulness.

1383—A test is given to Emma de Beston in Cambridge that is remarkably similar to tests given today to screen for early symptoms of Alzheimer's.

1600s—Forgetfulness is considered an unavoidable part of aging and the work of either witches or the devil.

1700s—Elderly people with dementia are hidden away or confined in hospitals for the insane, such as Bethlehem Royal (Bedlam) just outside London, England.

1838—French doctors suggest that changes in the minds of elderly people are caused by something different from what causes mental retardation and insanity, because the senile elderly had not been mentally retarded or insane before they became senile.

1907—Dr. Alois Alzheimer publishes "A new disease of the cortex," in which he describes the symptoms of a patient, Auguste D., who suffered amnesia, paranoia, and confusion. He also described what he saw when he autopsied her brain: Some brain cells were replaced by tangled masses, and others were coated with fatty deposits. Emil Kraepelin, a distinguished psychiatrist, proposes naming the new disease after Alois Alzheimer.

1900s-1960s—Alzheimer's disease is seen as a rare disease occasionally afflicting relatively young patients. Older patients with the same symptoms are said to have "senile dementia," thought to be something else entirely.

1968—G. Blessed, B. E. Tomlinson and M. Roth publish a paper in the *British Journal of Psychiatry* that first makes the connection between senile dementia and Alzheimer's, establishing that for the most part, they are the same disease.

1979—The Alzheimer's disease and Related Disorders Association, Inc. (Alzheimer's Association), holds its first official meeting and elects its first president.

1983—President Ronald Reagan approves the creation of a task force to oversee and coordinate scientific research on Alzheimer's disease.

1984—Research reveals the structure of beta-amyloid protein, the sticky substance that forms the plaques on brain cells that are typical of Alzheimer's disease.

1987—The gene responsible for amyloid precursor protein (APP) is sequenced. APP is broken down to form the beta-amyloid protein that forms Alzheimer's plaques.

1989—*The Journal of the American Medical Association* publishes a research paper that reports that Alzheimer's is more prevalent than previously thought. The National Institute on Aging releases revised figures, stating that approximately four million people are affected. The NIA warns that the number could grow to 14 million by the year 2050.

1991—The tau protein is identified as the main component of the tangles that are also seen in Alzheimer's patients' brains.

1993—The gene responsible for apolipoprotein E is sequenced. People with this gene have a higher risk for Alzheimer's disease.

1993—The U.S. Food and Drug Administration approves tacrine (Cognex®), the first drug for the treatment of Alzheimer's disease.

1995—Genetically engineered mice designed to contract a version of Alzheimer's disease are developed, improving the ability of researchers to study the disease.

1995—Donepezil hydrochloride (Aricept®) is approved by the FDA for the treatment of Alzheimer's disease.

1997—A population study shows that estrogen reduces the risk of Alzheimer's disease by more than 50 percent.

1997—Non-steroidal anti-inflammatory drugs, such as aspirin and ibuprofen, are linked with a 30 to 60 percent reduction in the risk of Alzheimer's disease.

1997—High dosages of Vitamin E show promise in slowing the progression of moderate Alzheimer's disease.

1997—Sixteen drugs in human testing are awaiting FDA approval.

1999—Scientists develop a vaccine that, in mice, appears to ward off the buildup of plaques on brain cells and even reduce the ones already present.

2000—The World Alzheimer's Congress 2000 is held in Washington, D.C., amid a new sense of optimism that effective treatment and/or prevention of the disease may not be many years away.

2000—Rivastigmine (Exelon®) is the third drug approved by the FDA specifically to treat symptoms of Alzheimer's disease.

2000—Human trials begin on a vaccine that appears to protect mice from the build up of plaques.

2001—The first human experiment in gene therapy for Alzheimer's is performed at the University of California, San Diego.

2001—Galantamine (Reminyl®) is the fourth drug approved by the FDA specifically to treat symptoms of Alzheimer's disease.

For More Information

Organizations

Alzheimer's Association
919 North Michigan Avenue
Suite 1100
Chicago, IL 60611-1676
Toll-free: (800) 272-3900
Phone: (312) 335-8700
Fax: (312) 335-1110
E-mail: info@alz.org

Alzheimer's Disease Education and Referral (ADEAR) Center
PO Box 8250
Silver Spring, MD 20907-8250
Toll-free: (800) 438-4380
E-mail: adear@alzheimers.org

Society for Neuroscience
11 Dupont Circle NW, Suite 500
Washington, DC 20036
Phone: (202) 462-6688

National Institute on Aging
Building 31, Room 5C27
31 Center Drive, MSC 2292
Bethesda, MD 20892
Phone: (301) 496-1752

Chapter Notes

Chapter 1. The Mind Thief

1. David L. Carroll, *When Your Loved One Has Alzheimer's: A Caregiver's Guide* (New York: Harper & Row, 1989), pp. 3–4.

2. Mary Norton Kindig, M.A., Molly Carnes, M.D., *Coping With Alzheimer's Disease and Other Dementing Illnesses* (San Diego: Singular Publishing Group, Inc., 1993), p. 2.

3. Gary D. Miner, Ph.D., Linda A. Winters-Miner, Ph.D., John P. Blass, M.D., Ph.D., Ralph W. Richter, M.D., Jimmie L. Valentine, Ph.D., Ed., *Caring for Alzheimer's Patients: A Guide for Family and Healthcare Providers* (New York: Plenum Press, 1989), p. 10.

4. Geoffrey Cowley, "Alzheimer's: Unlocking the Mystery," *Newsweek*, January 31, 2000, p. 46.

5. Associated Press, "As Alzheimer's Soars, Scientists Urge Attention to Disease's Early Signs," *The Dallas Morning News*, July 10, 2000, p. 3A.

6. Carroll, pp. 5–7.

7. J. Madeliene Nash, "The New Science of Alzheimer's: Racing Against Time—and One Another—Researchers Close in on the Aging Brain's Most Heartbreaking Disorder," *TIME* (Canadian Edition), July 17, 2000, pp. 34–35.

8. Cowley, pp. 48–49.

9. Associated Press, "FDA OKs New Alzheimer's Drug," MSNBC Web site, April 21, 2000, <http://www.msnbc.com/news/398318.asp> (April 22, 2000).

10. Cowley, p. 51.

11. Nash, p. 34.

12. "As Alzheimer's Soars, Scientists Urge Attention to Disease's Early Signs."

13. "General Statistics/Demographics," <http://www.alz.org/research/current/stats.htm> (July 27, 2000).

14. Ibid.

Chapter 2. The History of Alzheimer's Disease

1. John Medina, Ph.D., "What You Need to Know About Alzheimer's," <http://www.mhsource.com/catalog/alzpreview.html> (July 27, 2000).

2. Serita Corey, "Alzheimer's Disease: The Tragic Loss of Self, Anthropological Perspective," <http://www.umm.maine.edu/BEX/Lehman/HomePage.Stuff/text/beh450/SeritaCorey/scanthro.html> (July 27, 2000).

3. David Cassels, "Medical Monikers: A Name Not Easily Forgotten," *Medical Post*, Vol. 35, April 13, 1999.

4. "Alois Alzheimer," <http://www.alzwisc.org/alois.html> (July 27, 2000).

5. J. Madeliene Nash, "The New Science of Alzheimer's: Racing Against Time—and One Another—Researchers Close in on the Aging Brain's Most Heartbreaking Disorder," *TIME* (Canadian Edition), July 17, 2000, p. 34.

6. Alois Alzheimer, "A New Disease of the Cortex (Ger)," trans. E. Longar, <http://www.alzwisc.org/excerpt1.html> (August 9, 2000).

7. "Alois Alzheimer," <http://www.alzwisc.org/alois.html> (July 27, 2000).

8. Alzheimer.

9. Cassels.

10. Alzheimer.

11. Geoffrey Cowley, "Alzheimer's: Unlocking the Mystery," *Newsweek*, January 31, 2000, p. 48.

12. Nash, p. 34.

13. "Alzheimer's Disease/Alzheimer's Association Milestones," <http://www.alz.org/media/understanding/fact/milestones.htm> (July 27, 2000).

14. Ibid.

15. Cowley, p. 48.

16. Nash, pp. 36–37.

17. Ibid.

18. Ibid.

19. Maureen Reagan, "My Father's Battle With Alzheimer's," *Newsweek*, January 31, 2000, p. 55.

Chapter 3. What Is Alzheimer's Disease?

1. Gary D. Miner, Ph.D., Linda A. Winters-Miner, Ph.D., John P. Blass, M.D., Ph.D., Ralph W. Richter, M.D., Jimmie L. Valentine, Ph.D., Ed., *Caring for Alzheimer's Patients: A Guide for Family and Healthcare Providers* (New York, Plenum Press, 1989), pp. 219–223.

2. "Frequently Asked Questions," <http://www.alz.org/people/faq.htm> (July 27, 2000).

3. Cowley, pp. 48–49.

4. Nash, p. 38.

5. Cowley, pp. 48–49.

6. Nash, p. 37.

7. Cowley, pp. 49–50.

8. Nash, p. 38.

9. Mary Norton Kindig, M.A., Molly Carnes, M.D., *Coping With Alzheimer's Disease and Other Dementing Illnesses* (San Diego: Singular Publishing Group, Inc., 1993), p. 57.

10. Ibid.

11. Geoffrey Cowley, "Alzheimer's: Unlocking the Mystery," *Newsweek*, January 31, 2000, p. 48.

12. J. Madeliene Nash, "The New Science of Alzheimer's: Racing Against Time—and One Another—Researchers Close in on the Aging Brain's Most Heartbreaking Disorder," *TIME* (Canadian Edition), July 17, 2000, p. 39.

13. Ibid.

14. Kindig, pp. 58–59.

15. Cowley, p. 48.

16. Nash, p. 39.

17. Kindig, pp. 59–60.

18. Cowley, p. 48.

19. Nash, p. 39.

Chapter 4. Diagnosing Alzheimer's Disease

1. "Could It Be Alzheimer's Disease?" <http://www.alzheimer.ca/alz/content/html/media_en/wsigns-feature-eng.htm> (August 14, 2000).

2. Ibid.

3. "Diagnosis," <http://www.alz.org/people/understanding/diagnosis.htm> (July 27, 2000).

4. "Could it Be Alzheimer's Disease?"

5. Ibid.

6. "Ten Warning Signs," <http://www.alz.org/people/understanding/warning.htm> (July 27, 2000).

7. "Diagnosis."

8. Ibid.

9. J. Madeliene Nash, "The New Science of Alzheimer's: Racing Against Time—and One Another—Researchers Close in on the Aging Brain's Most Heartbreaking Disorder," *TIME* (Canadian Edition), July 17, 2000, p. 38.

10. "Diagnosis."

11. Ibid.

Chapter 5. Treatment of Alzheimer's Disease

1. Rebecca Goldsmith, "Alzheimer's Patients Fight 'The Long Goodbye,'" *The Star-Ledger*, February 13, 2000, pp. 1, 25.

2. "Treating Cognitive Symptoms," <http://www.alz.org/people/understanding/treatment/cognitive.htm> (July 27, 2000).

3. Ibid.

4. Geoffrey Cowley, "Alzheimer's: Unlocking the Mystery," *Newsweek*, January 31, 2000, p. 51.

5. "Treating Cognitive Symptoms."

6. Goldsmith, p. 24.

7. Ibid. as well as, p. 25.

8. "Just for You: What Can I Do?" <http://www.alzheimer.ca/alz/content/html/care_en/care-ihavead-whatcanido-eng.htm> (August 15, 2000).

9. "Treating Behavioral Symptoms," <http://www.alz.org/hc/treatment/behavior.htm>, (August 15 2000).

10. Ibid.

11. Ibid.

12. Mary Norton Kindig, M.A., Molly Carnes, M.D., *Coping with Alzheimer's Disease and Other Dementing Illnesses* (San Diego: Singular Publishing Group, Inc., 1993), pp. 219–222.

13. Ibid., p. 219.

14. 14. M. Sano, C. Ernesto, et al., The Members of the Alzheimer's Disease Cooperative Study, "A Controlled Trial of Selegiline, Alpha-Tocopherol, or Both as Treatment for Alzheimer's Disease," *New England Journal of Medicine*, April 24, 1997, pp. 1216–1222.

15. "Alternative Treatments," <http://www.alz.org/hc/treatment/alternative.htm> (August 15, 2000).

16. Ibid.

17. "Ginkgo Biloba," National Institute on Aging pamphlet, May, 1998, accessed at <http://www.alzheimers.org/pubs/gingko.txt> (July 27, 2000).

18. "Alternative Treatments."

19. Ibid.

20. Stephanie Allmon, "New Approach Emphasizes Choices for Alzheimer's Patients," *The Washington Times*, February 27, 2000, p. D4.

21. Claudia Kalb, "Coping With the Darkness," *Newsweek*, January 31, 2000, pp. 52–54.

Chapter 6. Social Implications of Alzheimer's Disease

1. "Alzheimer's Disease Statistics," <http://www.alz.org/media/understanding/fact/stats.htm> (July 27, 2000).

2. Ibid.

3. Ibid.

4. Ibid.

5. Ibid.

6. Ibid.

7. Tammy Sanner, "Back to the cradle," Roswell (N. Mex.) *Daily Record*, January 24, 1999, <http://www.roswellrecord.com/012499/news11.html> (July 27, 2000).

8. Karen Goldberg Goff, "Golden Years' Grinch," *The Washington Times*, May 9, 1999, p. D1.

9. Mary Norton Kindig, M.A., Molly Carnes, M.D., *Coping with Alzheimer's Disease and Other Dementing Illnesses* (San Diego, Singular Publishing Group, Inc., 1993), pp. 169–170.

10. David L. Carroll, *When Your Loved One Has Alzheimer's: A Caregiver's Guide* (New York: Harper & Row, 1989), pp. 176–177.

11. Kindig, pp. 172–173.

12. Ibid., pp. 174–175.

13. Ibid., pp. 175–181.

Chapter 7. Preventing Alzheimer's Disease

1. "Losing a Father to Alzheimer's Disease. . . Brendan Shanahan's Personal Story," <http://www.alzheimer.ca/alz/content/html/media_en/coffeebreak-feature-eng.htm> (August 14, 2000).

2. J. Madeliene Nash, "The New Science of Alzheimer's: Racing Against Time—and One Another—Researchers Close in on the Aging Brain's Most Heartbreaking Disorder," *TIME* (Canadian Edition), July 17, 2000, pp. 36–37.

3. Ibid.

4. Geoffrey Cowley, "Alzheimer's: Unlocking the Mystery," *Newsweek*, January 31, 2000, p. 50.

5. Ibid.

6. Ibid.

7. Ibid.

8. Sarah Parsons, "People From Large Families May Have Greater Risk of Alzheimer's," American Academy of Neurology press release, January 25, 2000, <http://www.eurekalert.com/releases/aan-plf012000.html> (August 17, 2000).

9. "On-the-Job Lead Exposure Could Increase Alzheimer's Risk," American Academy of Neurology press release, May 5, 2000, <http://www.sciencedaily.com/releases/2000/05/000505064307.htm> (August 17, 2000).

10. Charles Arthur, "Tell Me About It: Does Aluminum Cause Alzheimer's Disease?", *Independent*, June 8, 1998, p. 12.

11. "On-the-Job Lead Exposure Could Increase Alzheimer's Risk."

12. "Alzheimer's Disease: Glimmers of Hope," *Consumer Reports On Health*, April 2000, p. 4.

13. "An Active Life Helps to Ward Off Alzheimer's," American Academy of Neurology press release, May 8, 2000, <http://www.sciencedaily.com/releases/2000/000508082222.htm>, (August 17, 2000).

14. Ed Susman, "Study Supports Brain 'Workouts'," <http://www.msnbc.com/news/403599.asp> (August 17, 2000).

15. "Alzheimer's disease: Glimmers of Hope."

16. Ibid.

17. Ibid.

18. Susman.

19. "Alzheimer's Disease May be Lifelong Ill," *Capital Times* (Madison, Wis.), February 21, 1996, p. 5A.

20. "Alzheimer's Disease: Glimmers of Hope."

21. Ibid.

22. Ibid.

23. Cowley, p. 51.

24. "Estrogen Replacement Therapy Not Effective for Treatment of Alzheimer's Disease in Some Women," <http://www.alzheimers.org/nianews/nianews27.html> (August 17, 2000).

Chapter 8. Research and the Future

1. Warren Wolfe, "Alzheimer's: New Ways to Cope, but No Cure," *Minneapolis Star Tribune*, April 30, 1997, p. 8A.

2. "MRI May Prove Powerful Tool in Predicting Development of Alzheimer's Disease," <http://www.alzheimer's.org/nianews/nianews30.html> (August 17, 2000).

3. "Study hints at Alzheimer's vaccine," <http://www.msnbc.com/news/287560.asp> (January 1, 2000).

4. Laura Helmuth, "Alzheimer's Congress: Further Progress on a Beta-Amyloid Vaccine," *Science*, July 21, 2000.

5. Ibid.

6. Ibid.

7. Jeff Nesmith, "Potential Vaccine for Alzheimer's Safe for Humans," *The Palm Beach Post*, July 12, 2000, p. 3A.

8. Jean Marx, "Alzheimer's Congress: Drug Shows Promise for Advanced Disease," *Science*, July 21, 2000.

9. Charlene Laino, "Designer Gene May Fight Alzheimer's," <http://www.msnbc.com/news/235298.asp> (August 17, 2000).

10. Jeff Barnard, "Enzyme in Alzheimer's Onset ID'd," Associated Press, June 8, 2000.

11. Liza Jane Maltin, "Brain Scan May Be First-Ever Test for Alzheimer's, Could Mean Earlier Treatment, Prolonged Quality-of-Life," MSNBC Web site, n.d., <http://content.health.msn.com/content/article/1728.93161> (November 16, 2001).

Glossary

acetylcholine—A brain chemical that appears to be involved in learning skills and memory. People with Alzheimer's disease have a shortage of acetylcholine.

agitation—Disruptive vocal or motor behavior (screaming, shouting, complaining, moaning, cursing, pacing, fidgeting, wandering, etc.).

amyloid plaque—Abnormal cluster of dead and dying nerve cells, other brain cells, and amyloid protein fragments. Amyloid plaques are one of the abnormalities found in the brains of people with Alzheimer's.

amyloid precursor protein (APP)—A protein found in the brain, heart, kidneys, lungs, spleen, and intestines. The normal function of APP in the body is unknown. In Alzheimer's disease, APP is converted to beta amyloid protein, which forms plaques in the brain.

anti-inflammatory drugs—Drugs that reduce inflammation by modifying the body's immune system.

antioxidant—A substance that inhibits the actions of free radicals in the body. Vitamin E is an antioxidant.

antipsychotic—Medicines that reduce dopamine in the brain; These are sometimes called "major tranquilizers" or "neuroleptic" drugs.

apolipoprotein E-4 (ApoE4)—A protein that functions mainly to transport cholesterol that is associated with about 60 percent of late-onset Alzheimer's cases and is considered a risk factor for the disease.

APP—*See* amyloid precursor protein.

behavioral symptoms—Symptoms that relate to action or emotion, such as wandering, depression, anxiety, hostility, and sleep disturbances.

beta amyloid protein—A specific variation of the amyloid normally found in humans and animals. In Alzheimer's disease, beta amyloid becomes deposited in plaques in the brain.

cognitive abilities—Mental abilities such as judgment, memory, learning, comprehension, and reasoning.

cognitive symptoms—Symptoms that relate to loss of thought processes, such as learning, comprehension, memory, reasoning, and judgment.

combativeness—Incidents of aggression.

delusion—A false idea strongly maintained in spite of contradictory evidence.

dementia—The loss of intellectual functions (such as thinking, remembering, and reasoning) to the point that they interfere with a person's daily life.

enzyme—A protein produced by living organisms that promotes or otherwise influences chemical reactions.

Exelon®—*See* rivastigmine.

fibrils—Insoluble clumps of beta amyloid protein that cluster with other fibrils to form the plaques seen on the brain cells of Alzheimer's patients.

galantamine—One of the drugs approved for the treatment of Alzheimer's symptoms. It boosts the brain's supply of acetylcholine and enhances the receptiveness of brain cells to the chemical.

gamma secretase—Name given to the enzyme that creates beta amyloid from amyloid precursor protein. It has been tentatively identified as being the same as the protein Presenilin-1, already linked to early-onset Alzheimer's.

glutamate—A brain chemical normally involved in learning and memory. Under certain circumstances it can cause nerve cell death.

homocysteine—A blood compound linked to increased risk of Alzheimer's.

immune system—A system of cells that protect a person from bacteria, viruses, toxins, and other foreign substances.

late-onset Alzheimer's disease—The most common form of Alzheimer's disease, usually occurring after age 65.

late stage—The final stage in Alzheimer's disease, when symptoms have reached the point where the person can no longer care for himself.

magnetic resonance imaging (MRI)—A brain scanning technique that generates cross-sectional images of a human brain by detecting small molecular changes, and can distinguish between normal and abnormal tissue.

memantine—A drug currently in use in Germany to treat Alzheimer's disease. It makes brain cells less able to respond to glutamate. Oversensitivity to glutamate may damage the brain cells.

miroglia—Special immune system cells that try to clear away the amyloid plaques from the brains of Alzheimer's sufferers, but only succeed in damaging nearby healthy cells.

MRI—*See* magnetic resonance imaging.

mutation—A change in the genetic makeup of an organism.

nerve cell—The basic working unit of the nervous system. The nerve cell is typically composed of a cell body containing the nucleus, several short branches (dendrites), and one long arm (the axon) with short branches along its length and at its end. Nerve cells send signals that control the actions of other cells in the body, such as other nerve cells and muscle cells.

nerve growth factor—A protein that promotes nerve cell growth and may protect some types of nerve cells from damage.

neurofibrillary tangle—Accumulation of twisted protein fragments inside nerve cells. Neurofibrillary tangles are found in the brains of Alzheimer's patients.

neuron—*See* nerve cell.

neurotransmitter—A special chemical nerve cells use to send messages to each other.

Non-Steroidal Anti-Inflammatory Drugs (NSAIDs)—Drugs that reduce inflammation. Aspirin is one example.

pathology—The study of the changes produced by disease.

placebo—An inert/innocuous substance; for example, a sugar pill.

plaques and tangles—*See* amyloid plaque and neurofibrillary tangle.

presenilins—Proteins that may be linked to early-onset Alzheimer's disease. Presenilin-1 has been tentatively identified as the enzyme that creates beta amyloid from amyloid precursor protein.

proteins—The complex type of molecules out of which living tissue is formed.

rivastigmine—One of the drugs currently approved to treat the symptoms of Alzheimer's disease. It boosts the brain's supply of acetylcholine.

sundowning—Unsettled behavior of Alzheimer's patients evident in the late afternoon or early evening.

tacrine—One of the drugs currently approved to treat the symptoms of Alzheimer's disease. It boosts the brain's supply of acetylcholine.

tangles—*See* neurofibrillary tangles.

tau protein—The major protein that makes up neurofibrillary tangles found in degenerating nerve cells. Tau is normally involved in maintaining the internal structure of the nerve cell.

tissue—A group of similar cells that act together in the performance of a particular function.

toxin—A substance that can cause illness, injury, or death.

virus—An organism that is unable to reproduce on its own. Instead, it invades living cells and tricks them into producing hundreds of new viruses, which spill out when the cell dies and bursts.

vitamins—Various substances found in plants and animals that are required for life-sustaining processes.

wandering—Common behavior that causes people with dementia to stray and become lost in familiar surroundings.

Further Reading

James Lindemann Nelson, Hilde Lindemann Nelson, *Alzheimer's: Answers to Hard Questions for Families* (New York: Main Street Books, 1997).

Jennifer Hay, *Alzheimer's & Dementia: Questions You Have . . . Answers You Need* (Allentown, Pa.: People's Medical Society, 1996).

Margaret Shawver, Jeffrey K. Bagby (Illustrator), Jeff Bagby (Illustrator), *What's Wrong With Grandma? A Family's Experience With Alzheimer's* (Amherst, N.Y.: Prometheus Books, 1996).

Susan Dudley Gold, *Alzheimer's Disease* (Berkeley Heights, N.J.: Enslow Publishers, 2000).

Internet Addresses

Alzheimer's Association
<http://www.alz.org>

Alzheimer's Disease Education and Referral (ADEAR) Center
<http://www.alzheimers.org>

National Institute on Aging
<http://www.nia.nih.gov/>

Index